HOW TO DRAW HORSES

HOW TO DRAW HORSES

BY JOHN SKEAPING

Author and illustrator of
"Animal Drawing" (Studio)

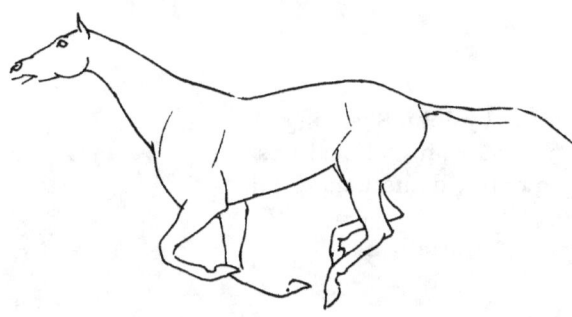

COACHWHIP PUBLICATIONS

Greenville, Ohio

CONTENTS

INTRODUCTION

WHEN I was a child, all vehicles were horse drawn, to-day these are almost as rare as motor cars were in those days; we take little notice of an everyday occurrence, but now that horses are almost a rarity we have become much more interested in them. Children know more about horses now than they did years ago when they could be seen about everywhere; the introduction of Pony Clubs and the many books on riding produced in recent years are, of course, partly responsible for this increase of knowledge.

I was quite old before I learned to ride; lack of opportunity and money were alone responsible for this delay. My one wish was to be a jockey; I was so obsessed with this idea that I spent most of my time pretending to be a horse, or drawing them. I drew horses from the age of three years onward, but I am sure I should never have done so had I possessed a real one of my own. It is far more important for would-be artists to possess a vivid imagination than any number of live horses.

I can remember following the farm carts for miles and miles watching every movement the horses made. I felt every effort in my own body and muscles; I imagined the bit in my mouth and could feel the tug of the reins in my cheeks. In this way I developed an understanding of horses from the emotional point of view, learning a great deal which could never have been taught to me by anyone.

Many teachers attach great importance to anatomy. Anatomical knowledge is useful but it can be acquired by anyone; to my mind it is of secondary importance to a real understanding of horses from the emotional point of view. By this I mean that which we feel and think about horses, our ideas; we all have different notions about the same things. Conversation would be very dull and tiresome if we only spoke of facts and never expressed our own ideas. It is just the same with drawing; if we are not expressing some idea in our work it is not worth doing and will be a bore to ourselves and everyone else.

There is a big difference between the outlook of children and adults. Children as a rule have more imagination than grown-up people, so children don't try to draw as adults do. You will be grown-up yourselves all too quickly and your chances of using your young and vivid ideas will by then have gone. Draw your horses in your own way, make them any shape and colour you think will look nice; red, green, anything you like. The horse you draw is an animal of your own creation; he can be made how you wish. The horse you ride must have good manners and nice comfortable paces; that is another matter, but the horse you draw cannot be ridden, so he can be wild, crazy or completely fantastic.

The drawings which I have done for this book are more or less like real horses; they are drawn so because I want to explain certain things about horses as well as about drawing.

JOHN SKEAPING

NOTES ABOUT RHYTHM

Condensed from the chapter in my book "Animal Drawing"

Before starting to draw a horse we must consider what is meant by Rhythm, a most important thing in art. It conveys ideas to us, and by its means we are able to convey ideas to other people.

Some people have a sense of rhythm as some have a sense of humour. It is difficult to acquire a sense of rhythm, but it can be done if approached correctly in the early stages of learning to draw. I can safely assume that most of you who are anxious to learn to draw have a sense of rhythm which stimulates the wish to make drawings of the animals you love and appreciate.

Let us analyse this question from another point of view. *Watch your horse walk along;*

notice the general time or tempo of his movement and draw a line which you feel best describes this motion.

Now he trots   *right to left*

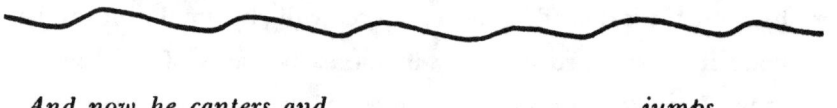

draw this in a similar manner

Now he canters

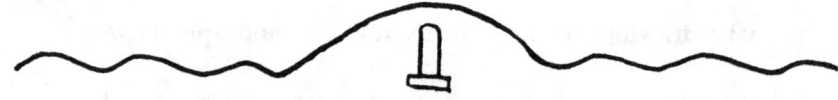

And now he canters and   *jumps*

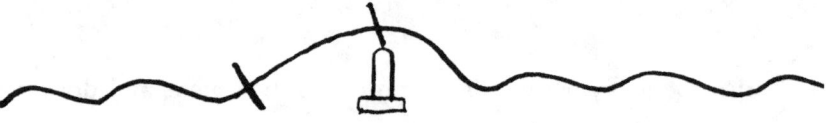

These lines represent the movement running through the axis of the animal. We will now apply this to the movement of a jumping horse, taking for our subject his descent marked off.

We are on the landing side of the jump; notice the general arc described in the movement of the horse as he comes over his fence to the ground. Draw this by itself at first.

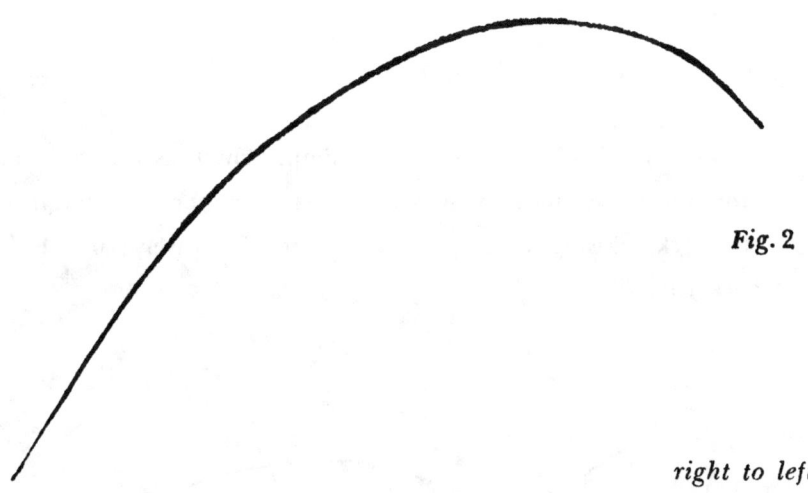

Fig. 2

right to left

Now watch him jump again and notice the answering rhythm or the line running along the underside of the neck and belly; put this in.

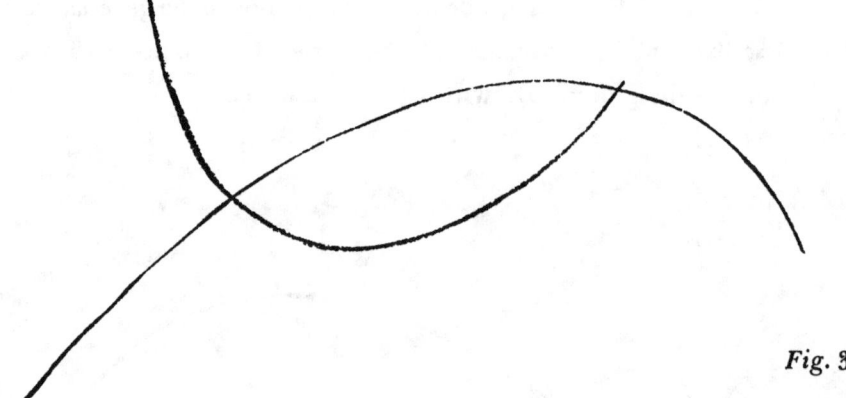

Fig. 3

Look for the longest and most simple rhythms all the time.
Now notice the movement which runs down the top margin of
the neck, passing through the body to the lower part of the
back leg.

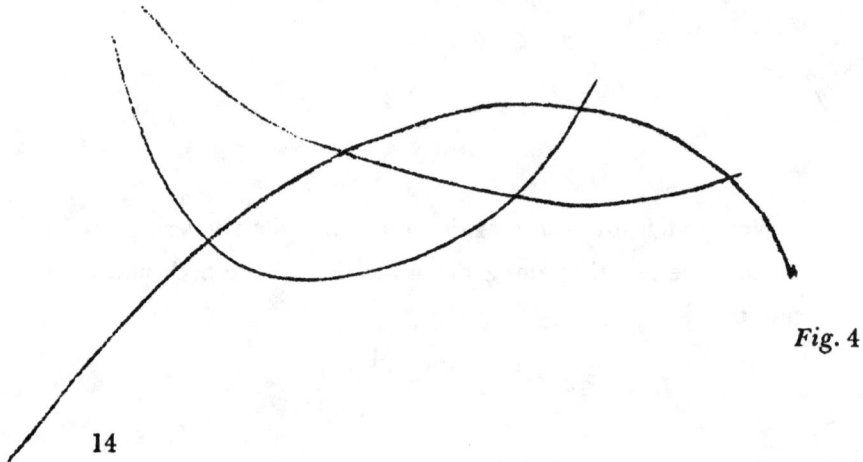

Fig. 4

14

These lines also represent three margins of the volume which we have drawn. If they are all in correct rhythmic harmony, the points at which the lines cross indicate the departure of the main forms creating the rhythm. Therefore, by this process, one automatically sub-divides the rhythms and movements; all the forms and minor forms thus fall in to their places directly contributing to, and supporting, the main movement of the whole animal.

Notice that the movement of both forelegs come out of the first line in like manner (Fig. 5).

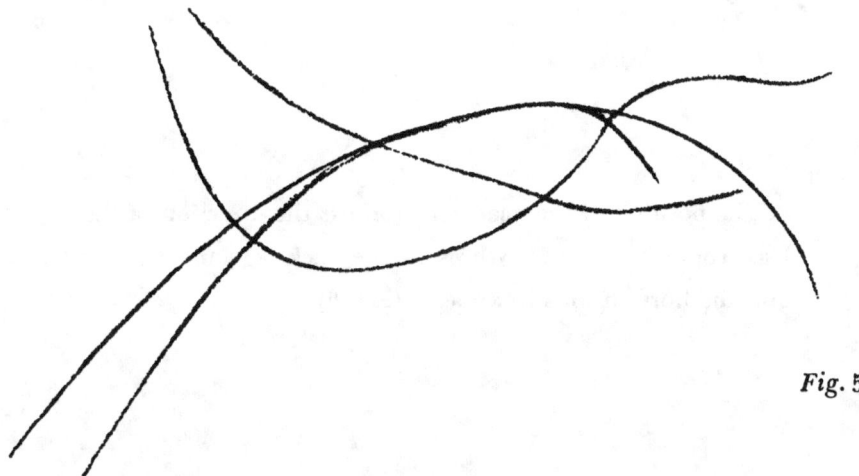

Fig. 5

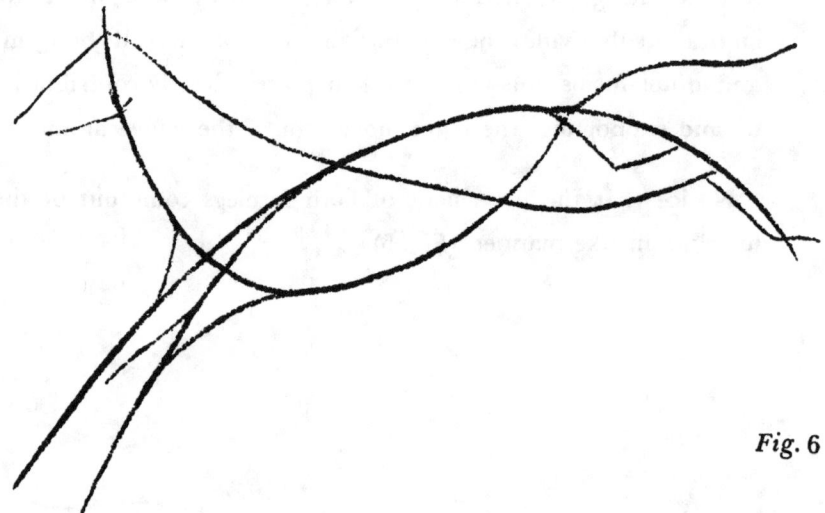

Fig. 6

The position of the head now follows the direction of the fore-legs; connect up the rhythms in the back legs and the forelegs, and the horse begins to appear (Fig. 6).

Continue the line of the horse's back to carry the movement through, into the neck and indicate the angle of the shoulder which runs from the base of the back of the neck to the commencement of the near foreleg. Your horse is practically complete (Fig. 7 and Fig. 8, over the page).

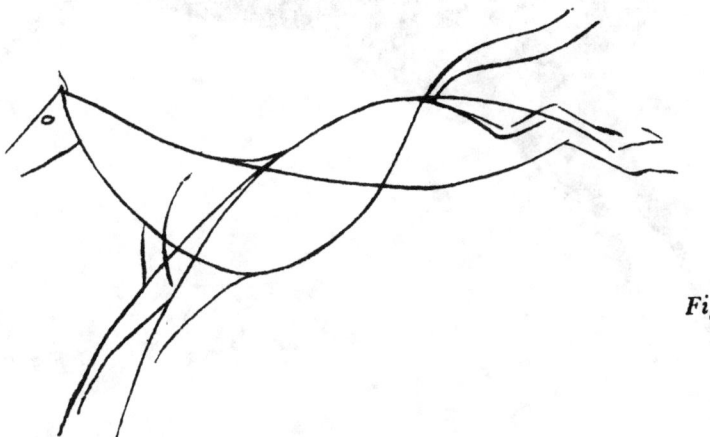

Fig. 7

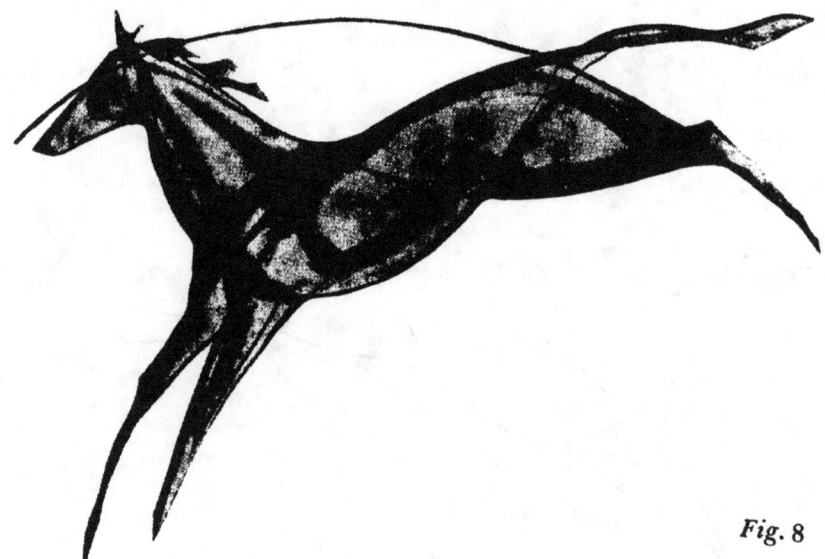

Fig. 8

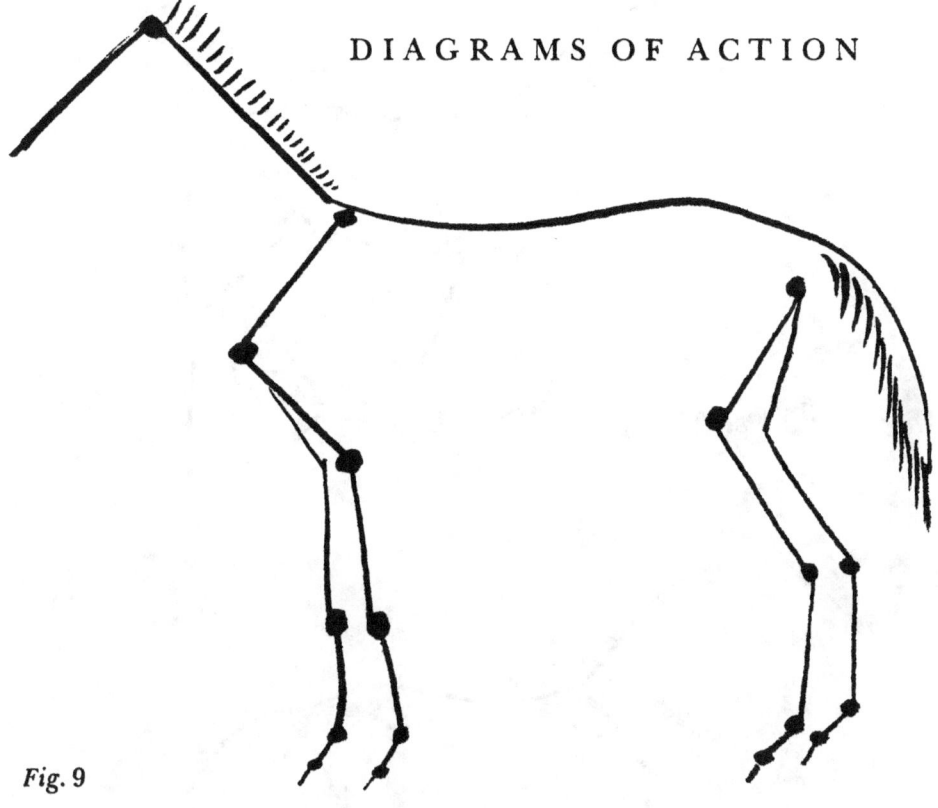

Fig. 9

Here are some simple diagrams showing the principal joints and their movements: (Fig. 9) Standing, (Fig. 10) Walking, (Fig. 11) Trotting, (Fig. 12) Cantering, (Fig. 13) Galloping. (Figs. 14, 15, 16, 17) show the principal joints and movements of the rider in conjunction with the horse in the four actions of Walking, Trotting, Cantering and Galloping.

19

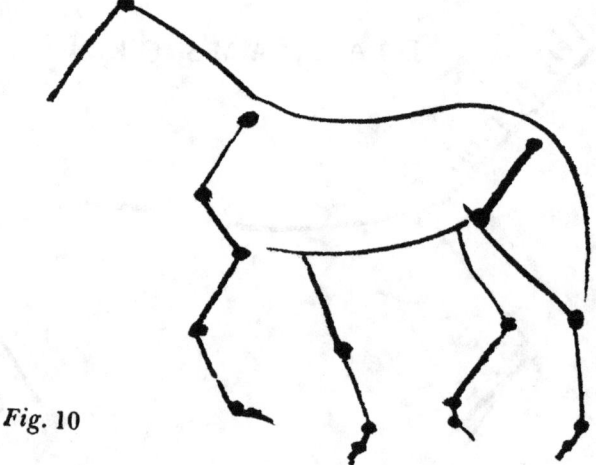

Fig. 10

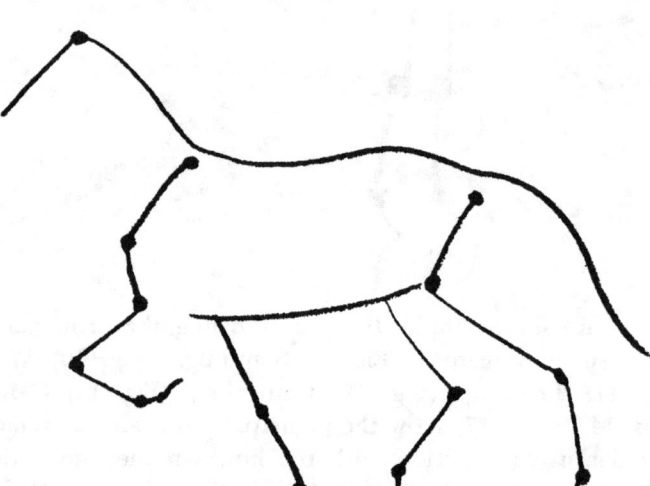

Fig. 11

20

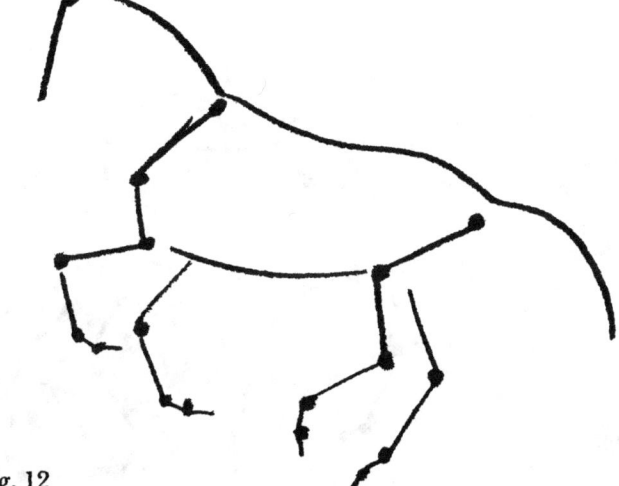

Fig. 12

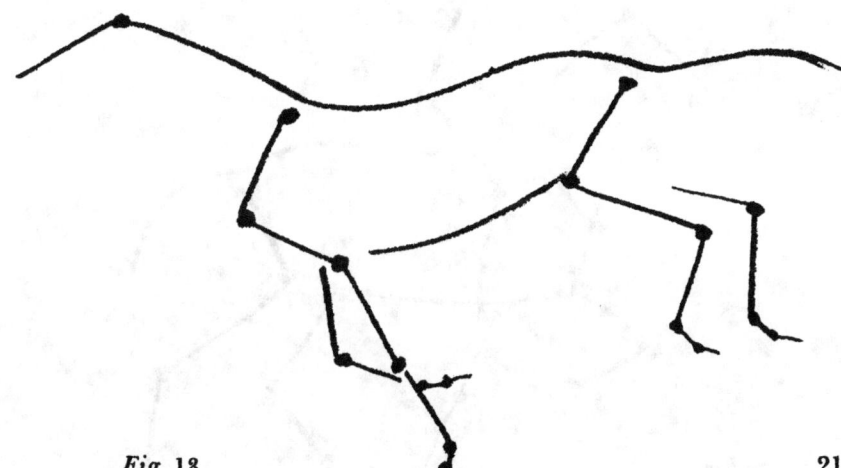

Fig. 13

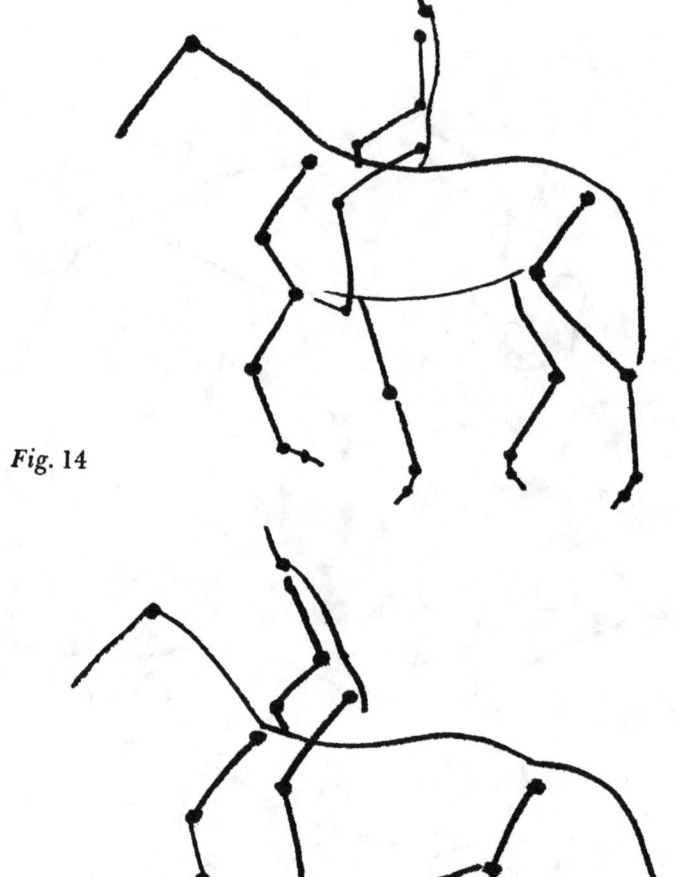

Fig. 14

Fig. 15

22

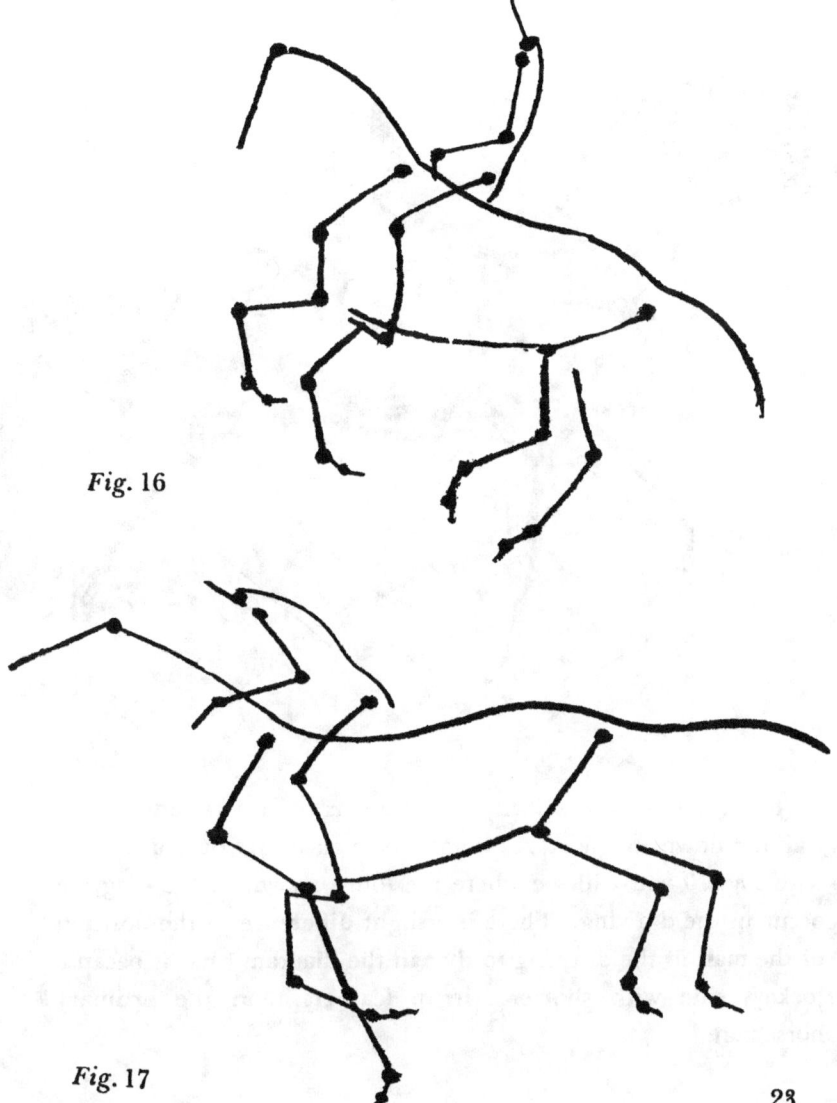

Fig. 16

Fig. 17

23

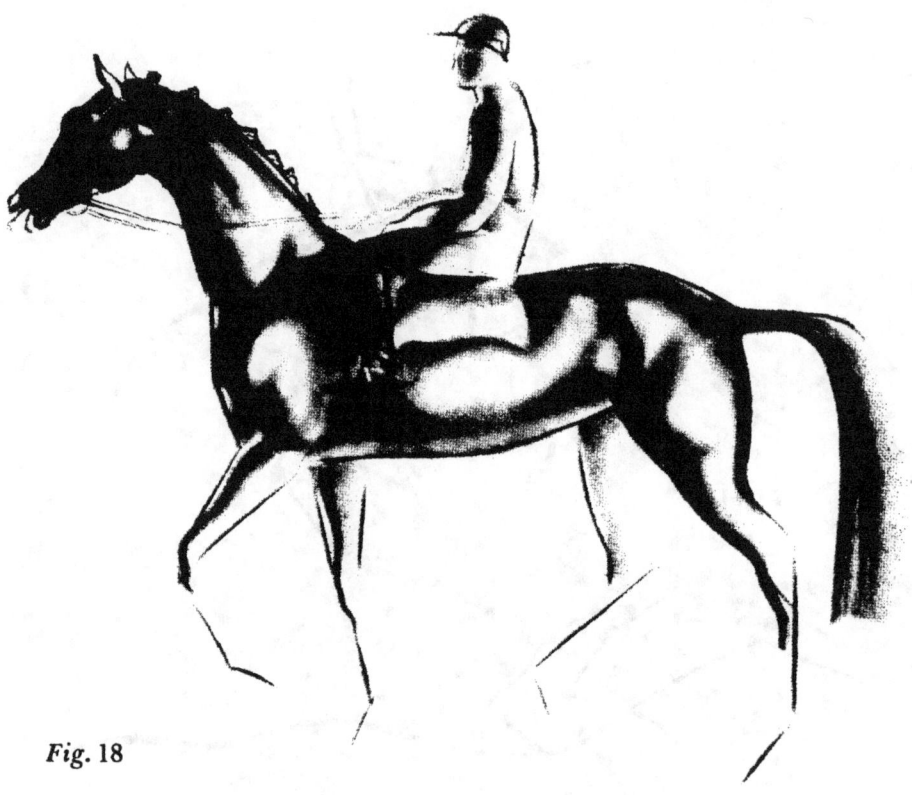

Fig. 18

(Fig. 18) This is one of my own drawings of a horse and jockey walking down to the starting gate for a race. If you compare it with Fig. 10 you will see where the joints shown in the diagram occur in the drawing. There is a slight difference in the position of the man in the drawing to that in the diagram, that is because jockeys ride with shorter stirrup leathers than the ordinary horseman.

24

(Fig. 19) The position of this drawing is also different from that of the diagram (Fig. 12) showing a horse at the canter. This horse is cantering, but the position is foreshortened, that is, going away from you, but reference to the diagram will show you where the joints occur in this drawing. These charts are just to guide you; they are not intended for copying.

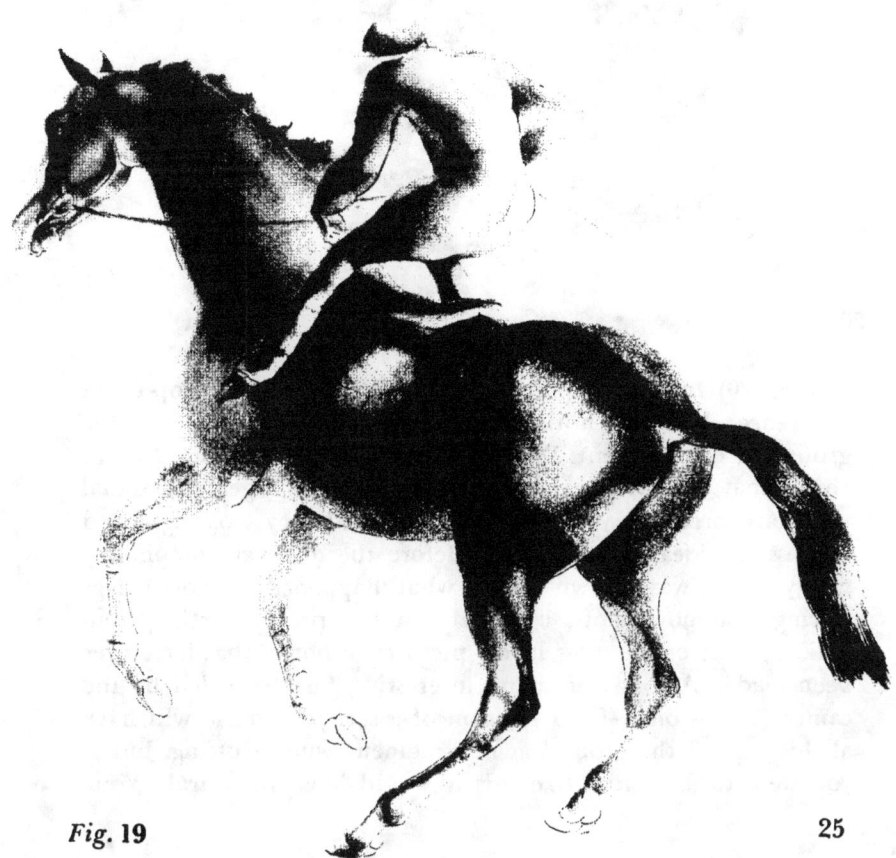

Fig. 19

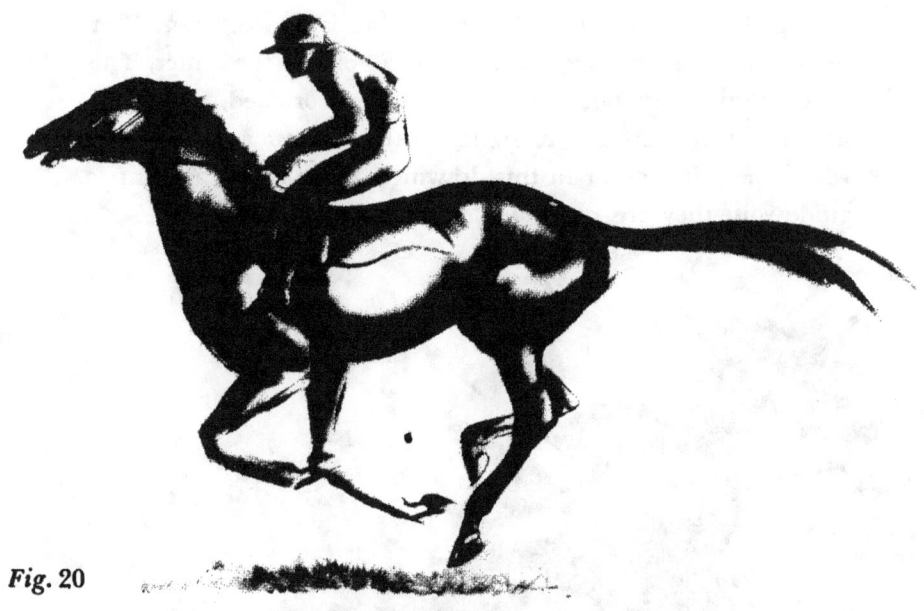

Fig. 20

(Fig. 20) In this adaptation of Fig. 13 there is an important difference. You will notice that all the horse's feet are off the ground at one moment. Whilst this is an important fact, I don't think that it matters very much if you don't get the actual positions correct in your drawings provided they look right and express the idea of movement. Before the discovery of photography, little was known about what happened to horses legs during fast movements, but that did not prevent artists from making some of the most lovely pictures of horses that have ever been made. Among the many interesting facts revealed by the camera is this one:—for a fraction of a second a horse will have all his legs off the ground at one moment when trotting, but if you were to draw him like this it would look unnatural. Your

26

job is to make your drawings look right, so don't be dominated by actuality.

(Fig. 21) Whilst we are discussing facts concerning the movements of horses here is a drawing of a trotting horse which shows him ambling or moving both legs forward on the same side together. Whilst this action is peculiar to some horses, the Camel and Blackbuck always walk in this fashion; among the various breeds of dogs this way of walking is frequently adopted by Greyhounds. It is not a nice action in any animal as it causes the body to roll from side to side in a rather ungainly manner.

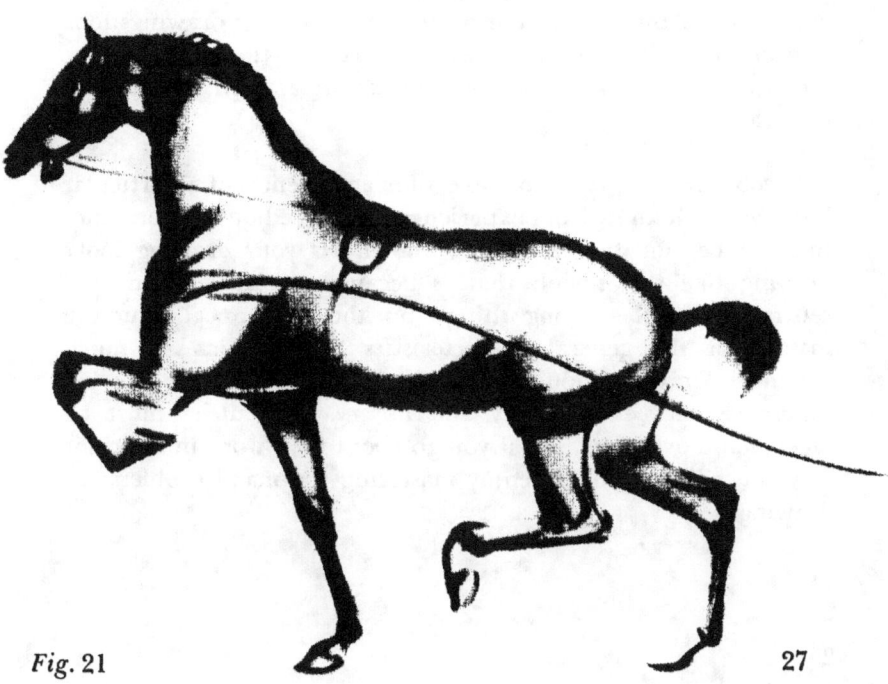

Fig. 21

What interests me are the unusual movements made by horses when frightened, enraged, or when they are making some violent effort (Fig. 22). I made this drawing of two Dartmoor Pony Stallions fighting; this is indeed an unusual sight, and I may tell you it is most alarming being as near to them as I was. They plunge down on their knees and try to bite the forelegs of their opponent and then rear into the air striking at each other's heads with their forelegs. In contrast to the violent movements of the ponies (Fig. 23) these racehorses lining up for the start are very quiet, but there is an expression of an excitement of a more subtle nature, a nervous tension as they are held back by the jockeys.

Your capacity as an artist will be measured by your power to express ideas and not by your ability to make your drawings look like photographs of horses. The character of the animal is the all-important thing; exact representation is well left to the camera.

If you have ever tried to make an exact likeness of a particular horse you will know from experience what a tedious performance this can be, and how after all your efforts your drawing looks nothing like the model; that is because you have been concentrating on the wrong things, on the anatomical structure instead of the general characteristics upon which so much depends. Drawing should always be great fun. There is a big difference between difficulty and misery. Difficulties must be tackled and overcome, but if you go about your work in the right way you will thoroughly enjoy mastering the many problems of drawing.

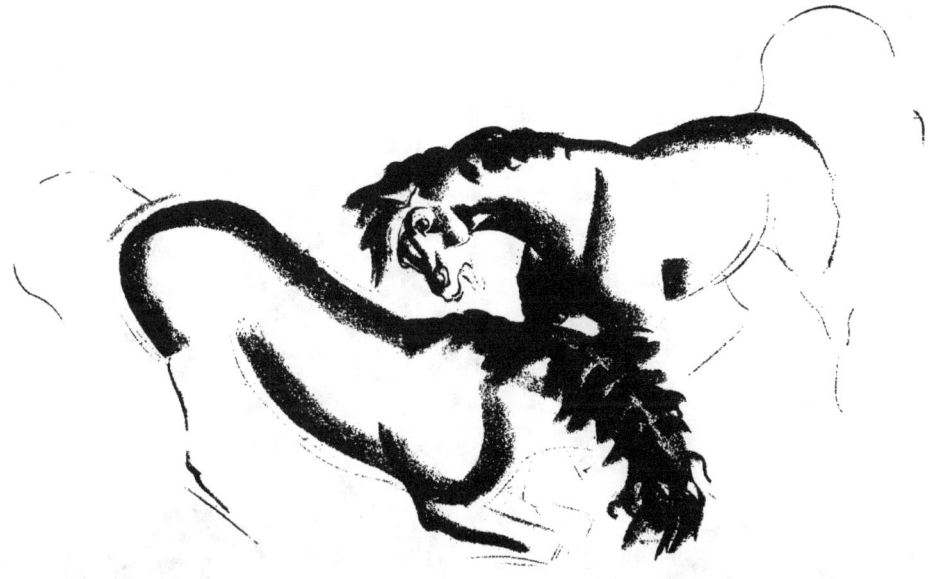

Fig. 22

Fig. 23

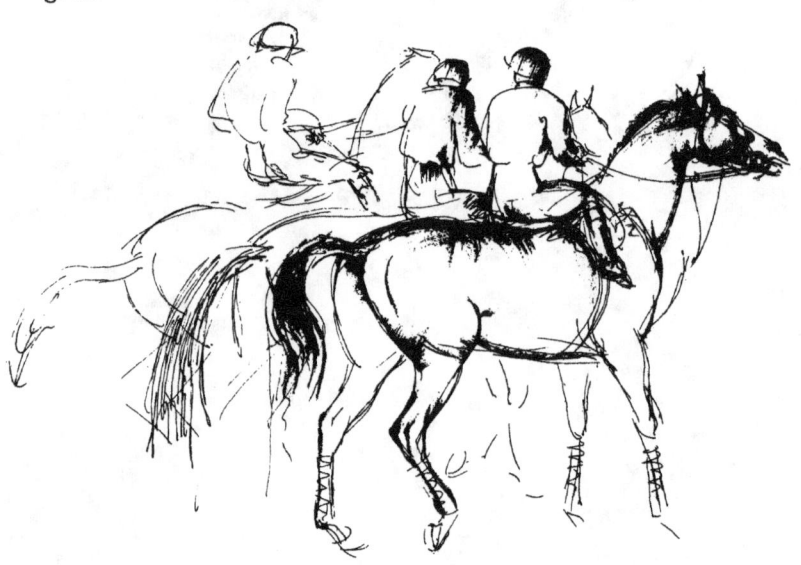

THE USE OF MATERIAL

Pencil, pen and ink, coloured pencils, chalk, wax crayons, conte crayon, natural earth chalks, pastels and charcoal. These are some of the many things with which you can draw. There is an infinite variety of papers for your use; always have a good selection of materials around you. Some of the nicest papers for drawing are quite cheap, such as sugar paper and lining paper. The only disadvantage about cheap white paper is that it quickly discolours when exposed to the light, and the drawings fade in a short time.

For sketching out of doors I advise you to use an easily controlled medium, such as a pencil or conte crayon, something that will not smear when the wind blows your paper about. When you can work on a table at home, you can have all your different materials spread out before you, and can use several different things on one drawing; for example, pen and ink with chalk, or pen, pastel and conte crayon.

If you take my advice you will do most of your drawing at home, where you can sit at a table quite undisturbed and concentrate fully on what you are doing. In this way you will train your memory and imagination, so that when you do see real horses out of doors you will be able to learn the most important things about them from observation alone. Of course, if there is some particular thing that you want to know, you can make a drawing from the living animal concentrating on that problem alone, but your complete pictures must be drawn from memory and imagination.

31

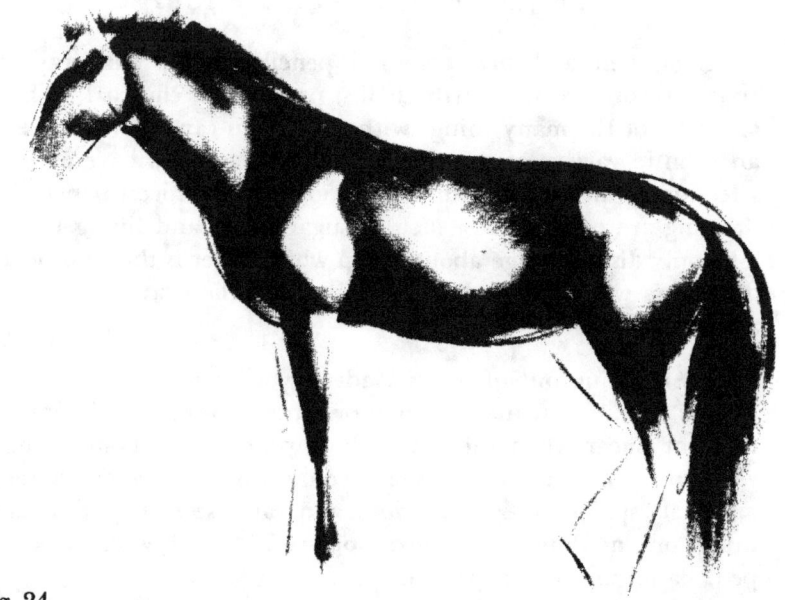

Fig. 24

(Fig. 24) This is a drawing made from a Dartmoor Pony. I wanted to see what happened to his body and tail when resting on one back leg. Horses frequently rest in this manner, but they have a nasty habit of moving from the position in which you want them to remain as soon as you start to draw. Having caught the pony in this position, no time was to be lost, so I used a soft brown chalk because it covers more space in less time than a pencil. It may not be so good for detail, but chalk is an excellent material for getting an idea on to paper in the least possible time; it will smudge, of course, but in this case smudging did not matter.

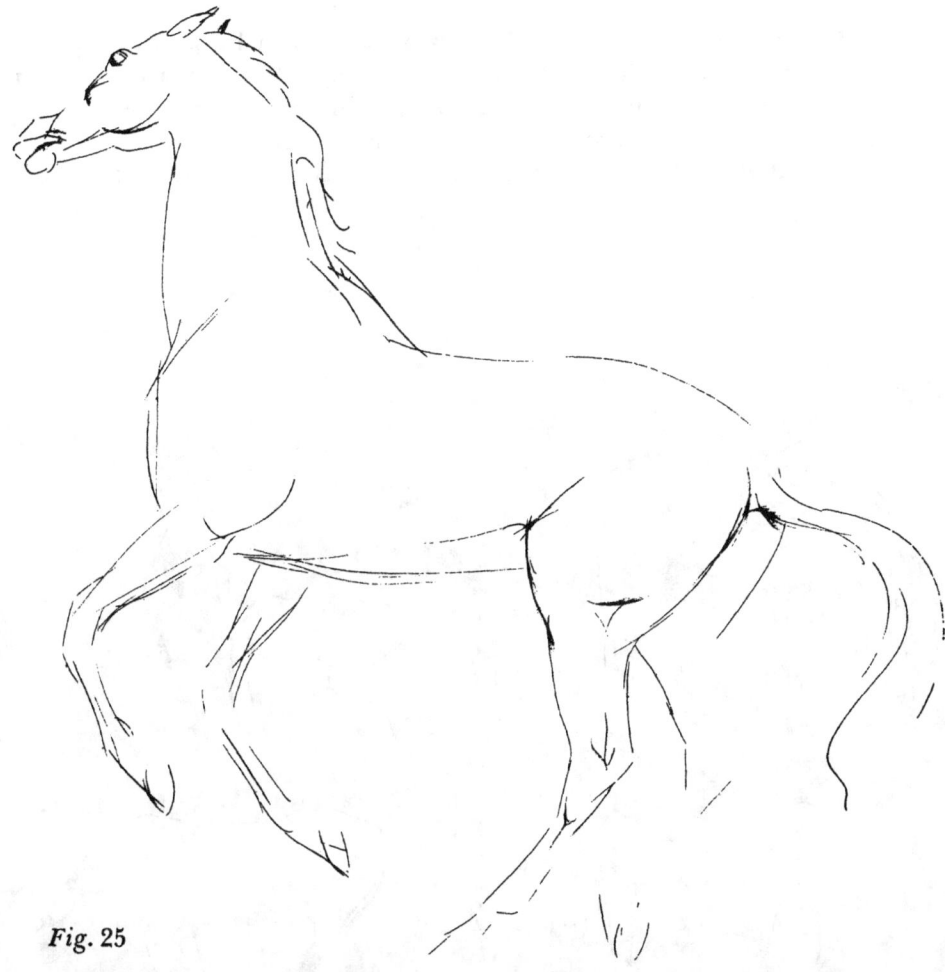

Fig. 25

(Fig. 25) If you want fine detail you can use a pen as employed in this drawing, or it can be used for putting down quickly the general shape and movement.

Figs. 26-7 are some quick sketches made from a horse which got into my garden from the next field. You will notice a blot on one of the drawings; ink will blot and smear too; very well, make use of this peculiarity. You see I have deliberately smudged the ink for the tails and manes, as well as in other

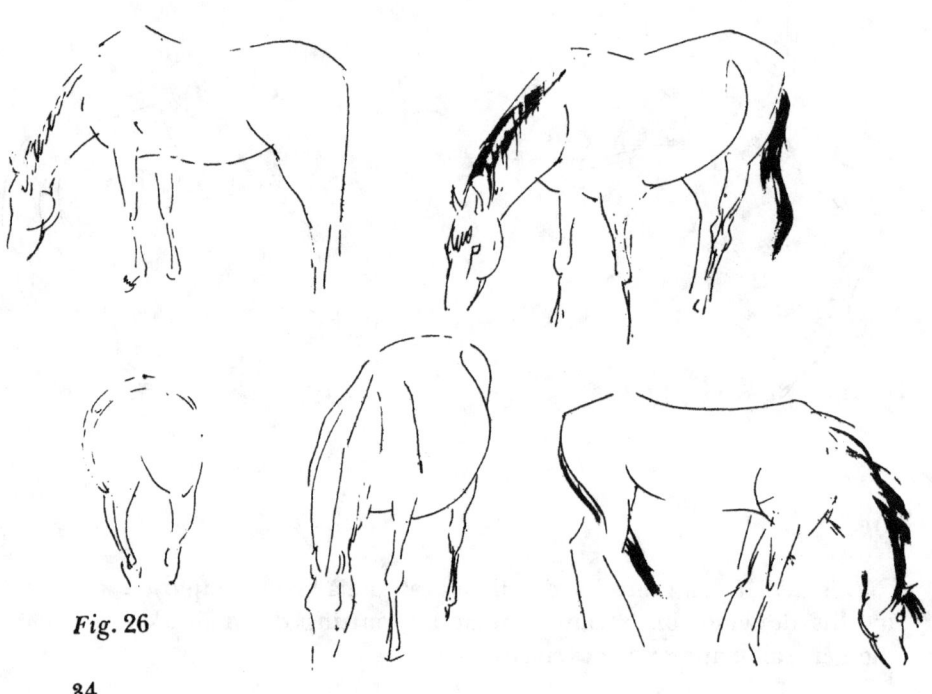

Fig. 26

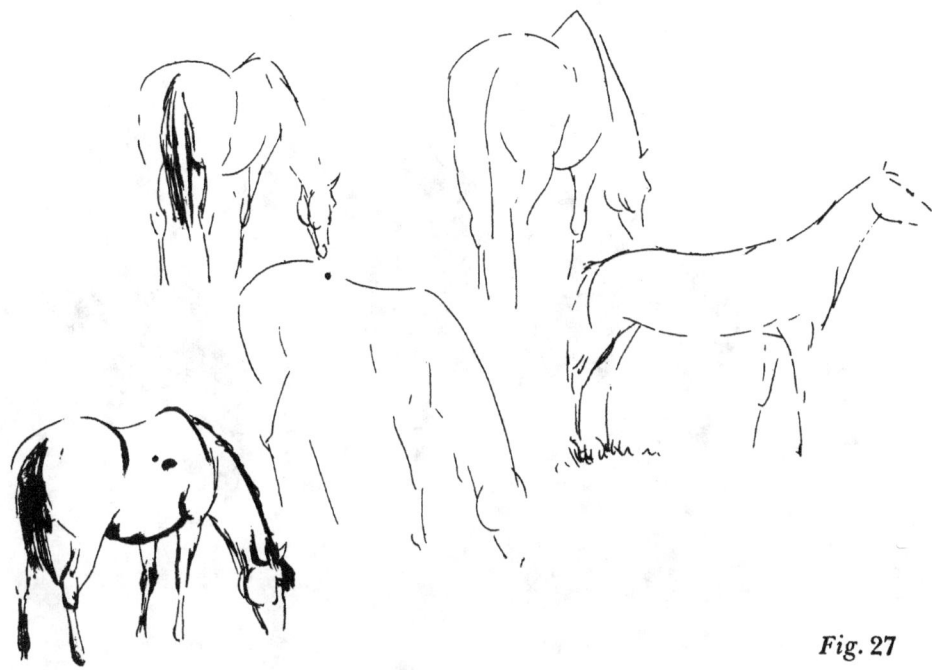

Fig. 27

places, to strengthen the forms; by doing this I can turn this sometimes nasty habit of the material to good account. Had I not made the blot on the horse accidentally, I might not have thought of using ink in this way. Many useful things have been discovered by accident; that is where imagination plays yet another important part in drawing.

Fig. 28

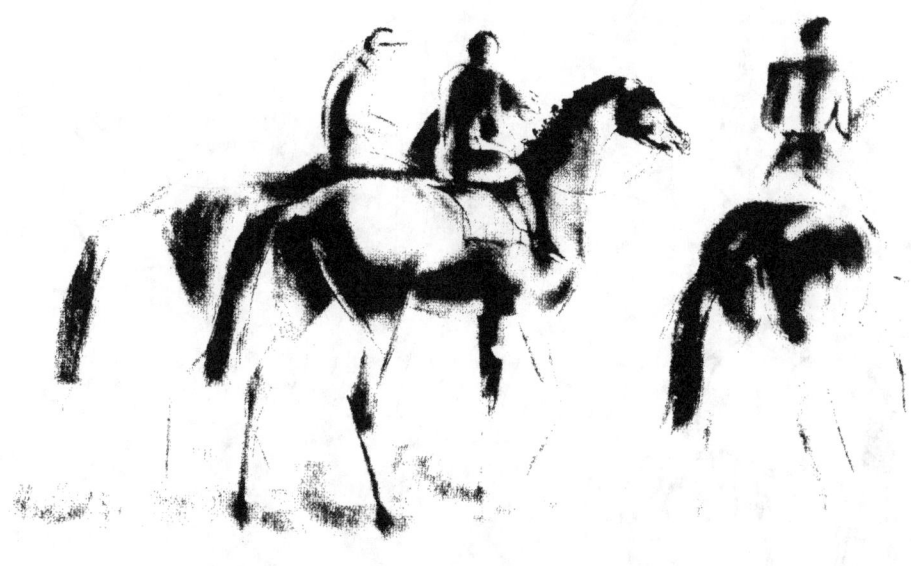

Soft pastel smudges very easily. (Fig. 28) These racehorses are drawn almost entirely by smearing the pastel on with my fingers. Where it was necessary to define more clearly certain of the forms I have used a pen and ink. If you understand thoroughly the limitations of your mediums, and you possess a good variety of drawing materials, you can use several different ones on the same work to enable you to achieve the desired effect. (Fig. 29)

36

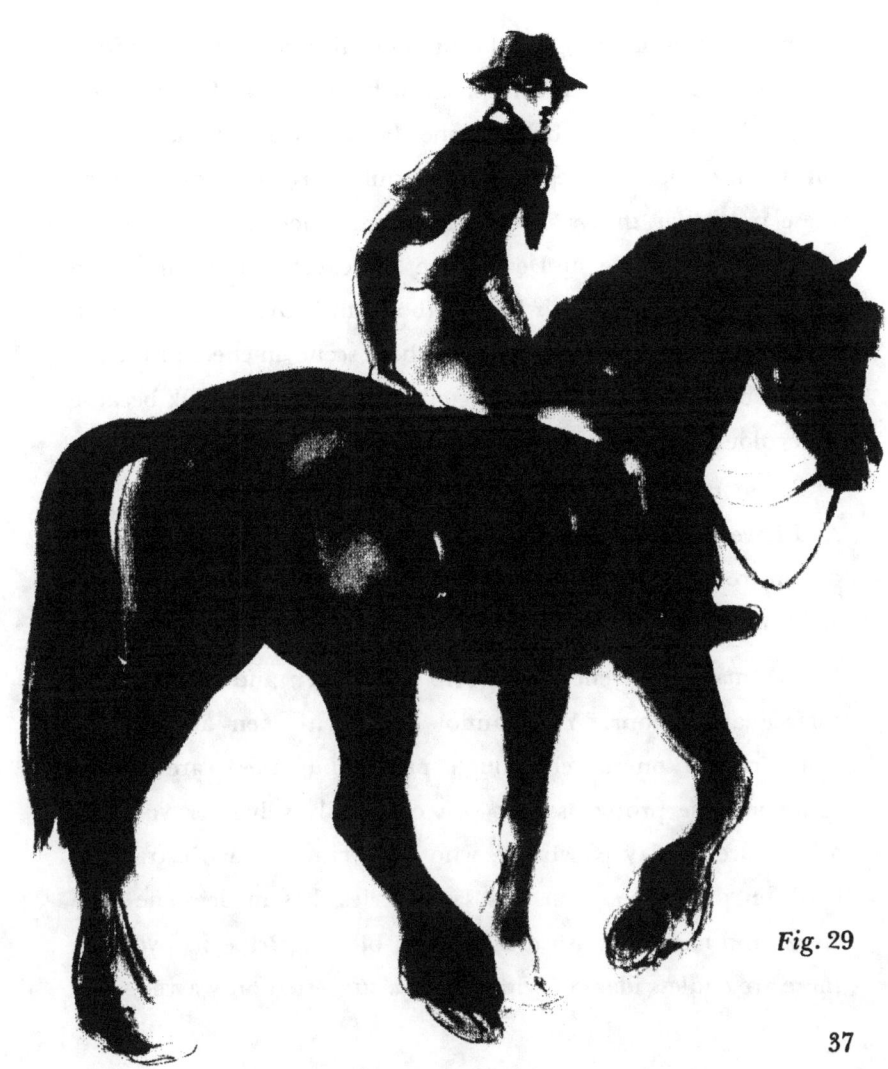

Fig. 29

In making this drawing of a farmer and his horse returning from work I have used three things, a red brown chalk for the main shapes, black conte crayon to define the big forms, and a pen and ink for the detail. These are the technical reasons for selecting these particular things. Then there are other reasons. For example, where I live in Devonshire the earth is red, and when dried by the hot sun it is blown about and covers the men and horses in fine red dust, giving the whole scene an effect of intense heat. For this reason also I selected this red brown chalk because this colour helped to express the idea of heat.

Try to think of fresh combinations of materials for yourself. As I have said, the advantage of having all your materials spread out in front of you is that they will suggest all kinds of new and exciting ideas.

The main differences between one paper and another are surface and colour. You cannot draw with pen and ink or conte crayon on a very rough paper, but these are simple common-sense problems that you can easily solve for yourself. Mrs. Clare Turlay Newberry, who has written and illustrated a book on drawing cats in this same series, has made some very clever and effective wash drawings on blotting paper; so you see there are endless ideas of which I have suggested only a very few.

DRAWING FROM LIFE

The next six drawings are all studies of the same horse. The first of these is a drawing of the head alone (Fig. 30). The disposition and proportion of the forms are rather complicated, so I have made a simple geometric diagram which may help you to realize the general construction of a horse's head (Fig. 30A). When I started the drawing (Fig. 30) he was resting under some trees, but when this drawing was finished he showed no signs of moving away, so I started off again to draw the whole of him (Fig. 31). The first attempt went wrong. I never use an india-rubber, because if you rub out mistakes it is difficult to remember where you went wrong, and you are liable to repeat them. Keep the bad drawing in front of you and start again. You will learn more from your failures than from your successes. Draw quite freely and let the result take care of itself. (Fig. 32) The second attempt is much better. Checking up on the first drawing I could see where I went wrong thereby avoiding the mistakes of the first effort.

(Figs. 33-4) Now the horse moved away and commenced grazing, wandering slowly away, changing his position all the time. I could only make just quick sketches of him with a pencil. When drawing with a pencil use a B. or BB., and don't make a hard line round the outside of the forms; draw on the forms themselves.

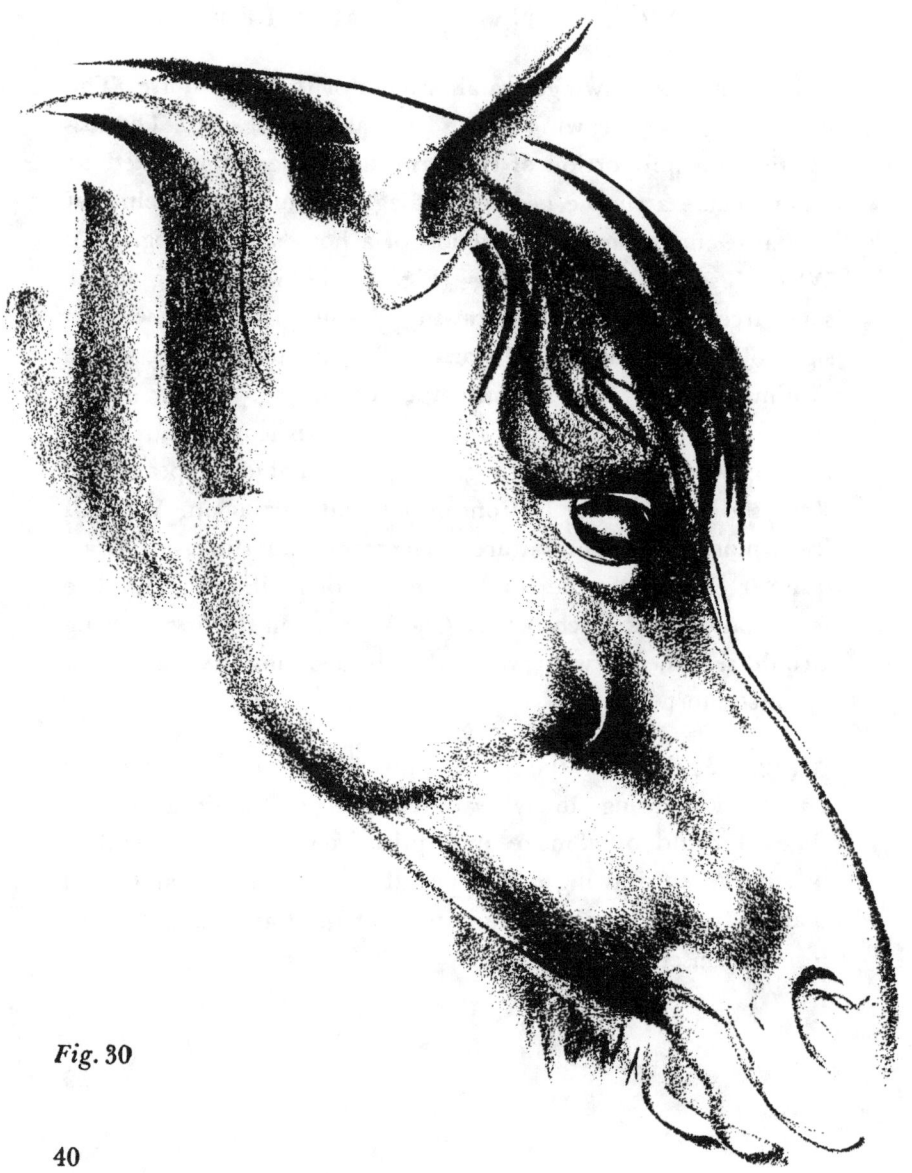

Fig. 30

40

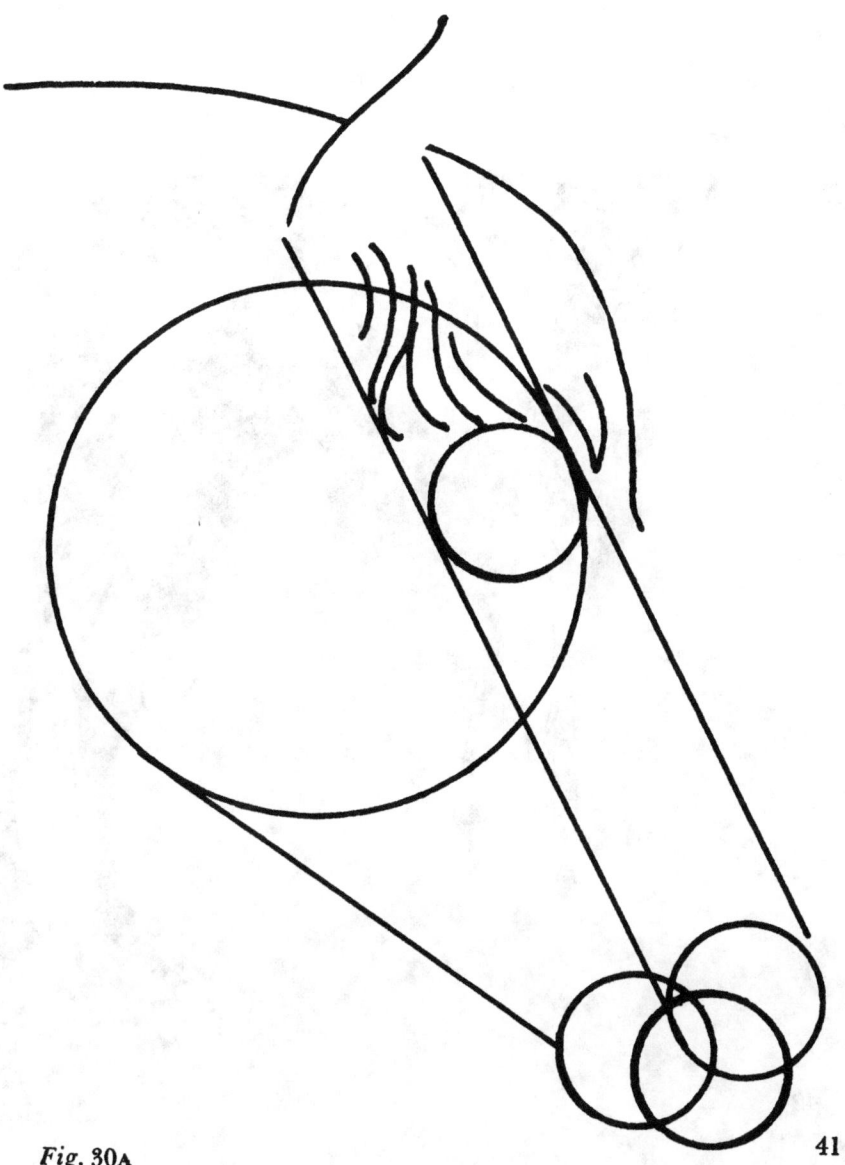

Fig. 30A

41

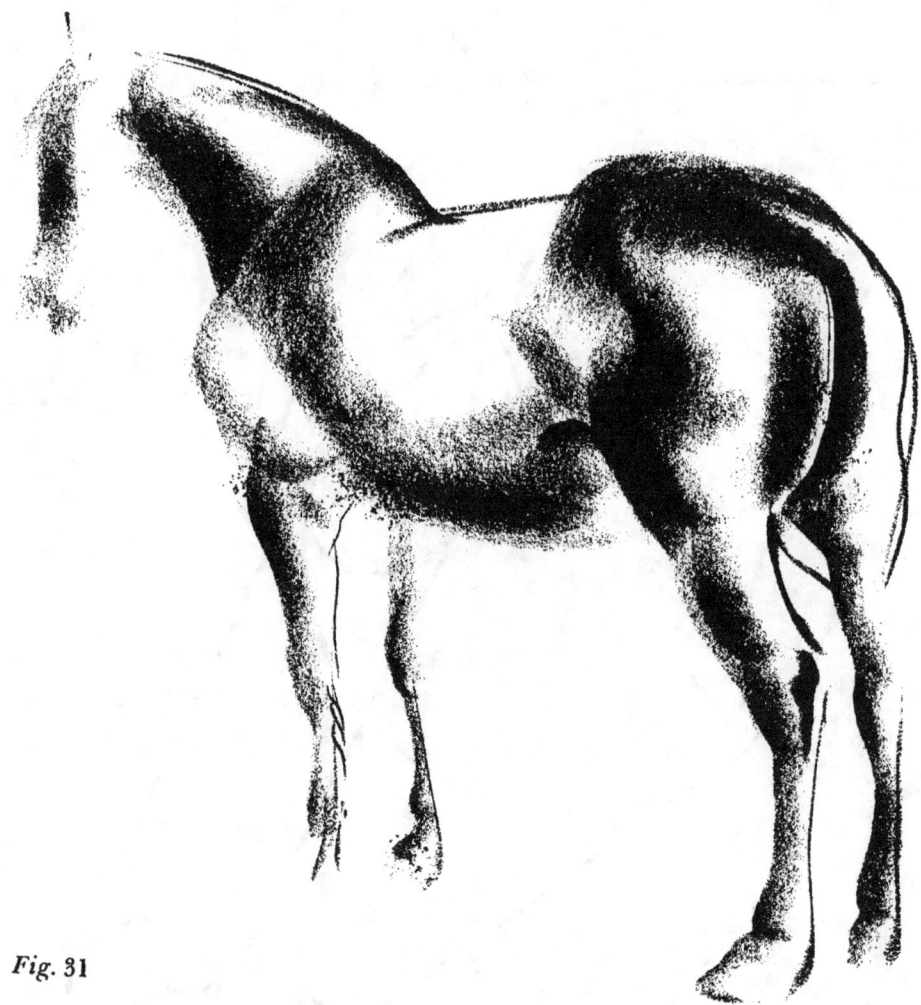

Fig. 31

42

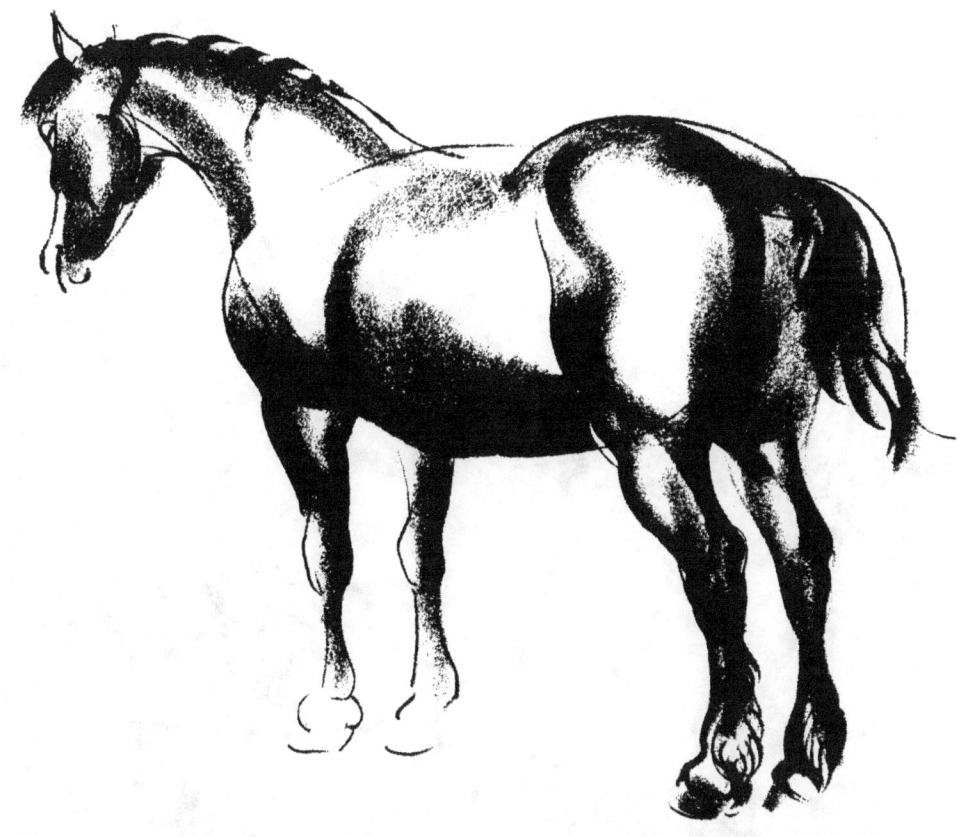

Fig. 32

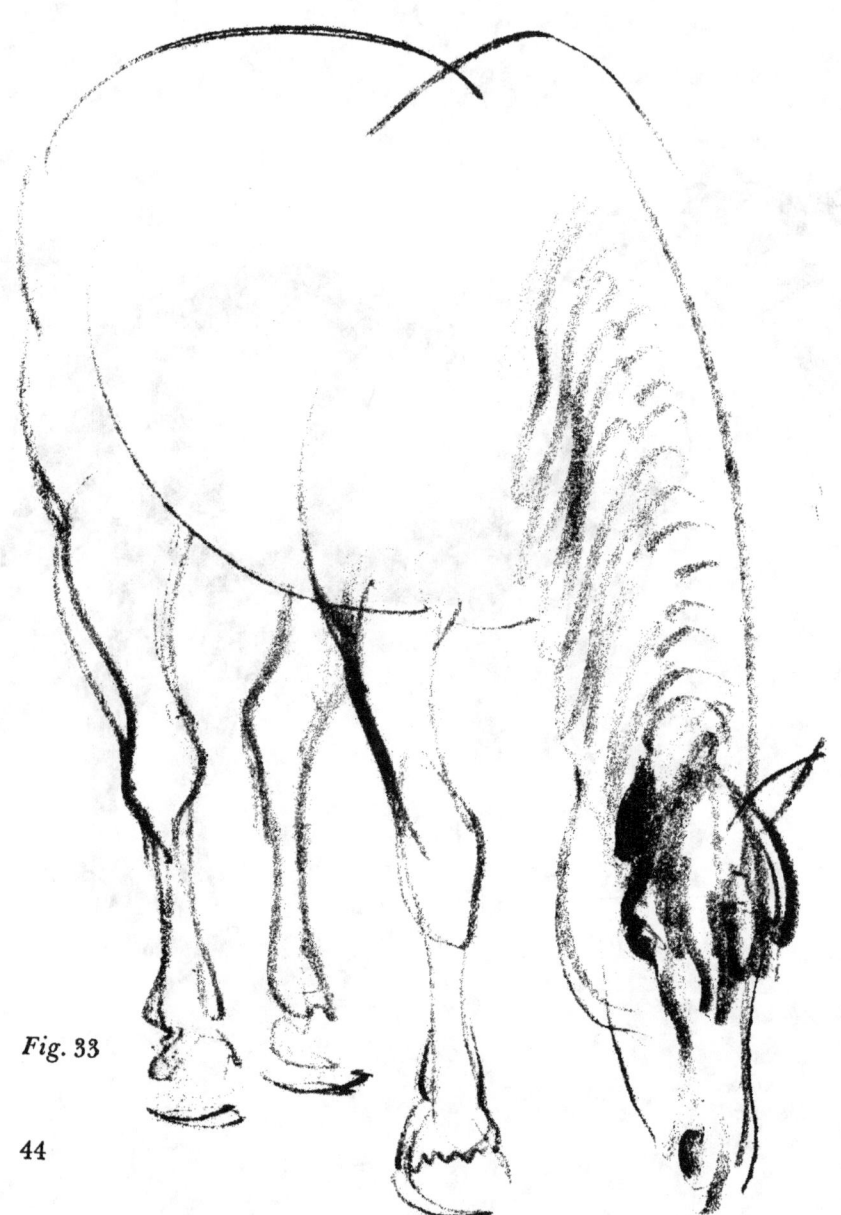

Fig. 33

44

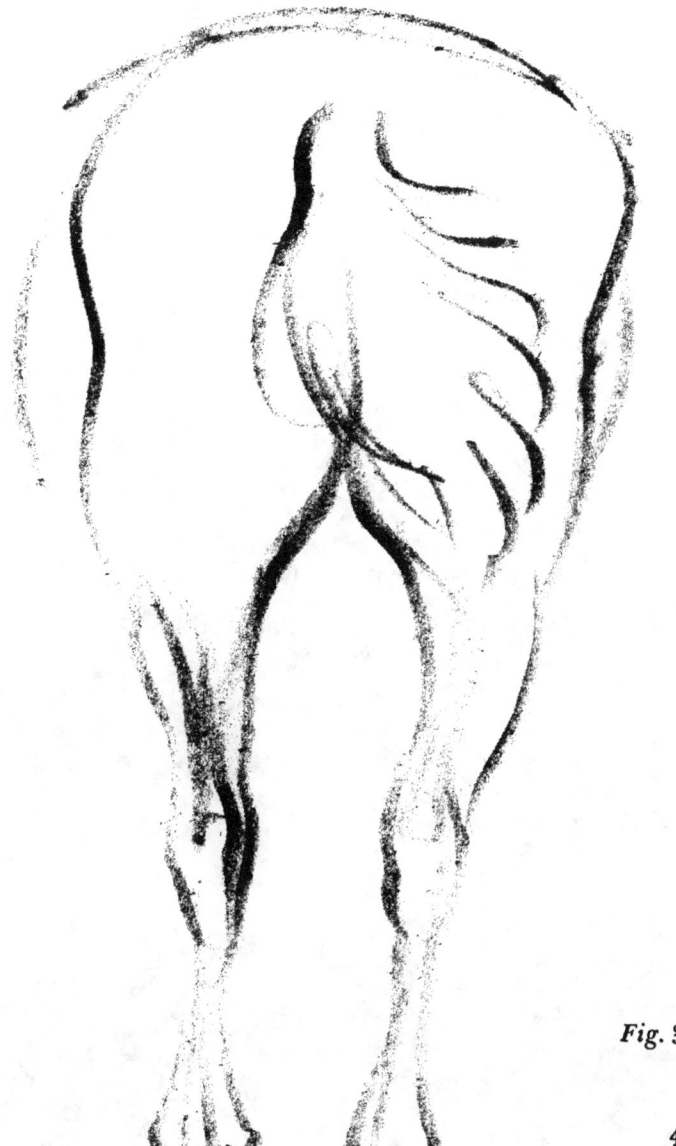

Fig. 34

45

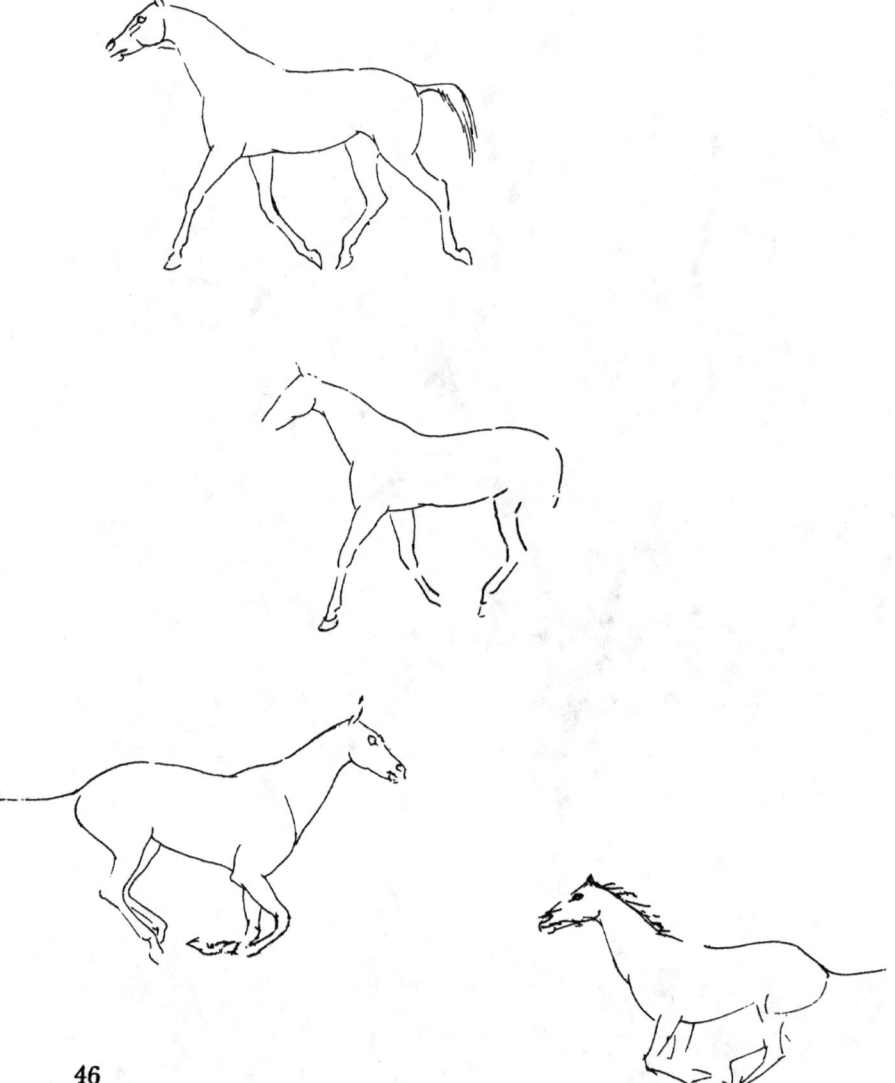

46

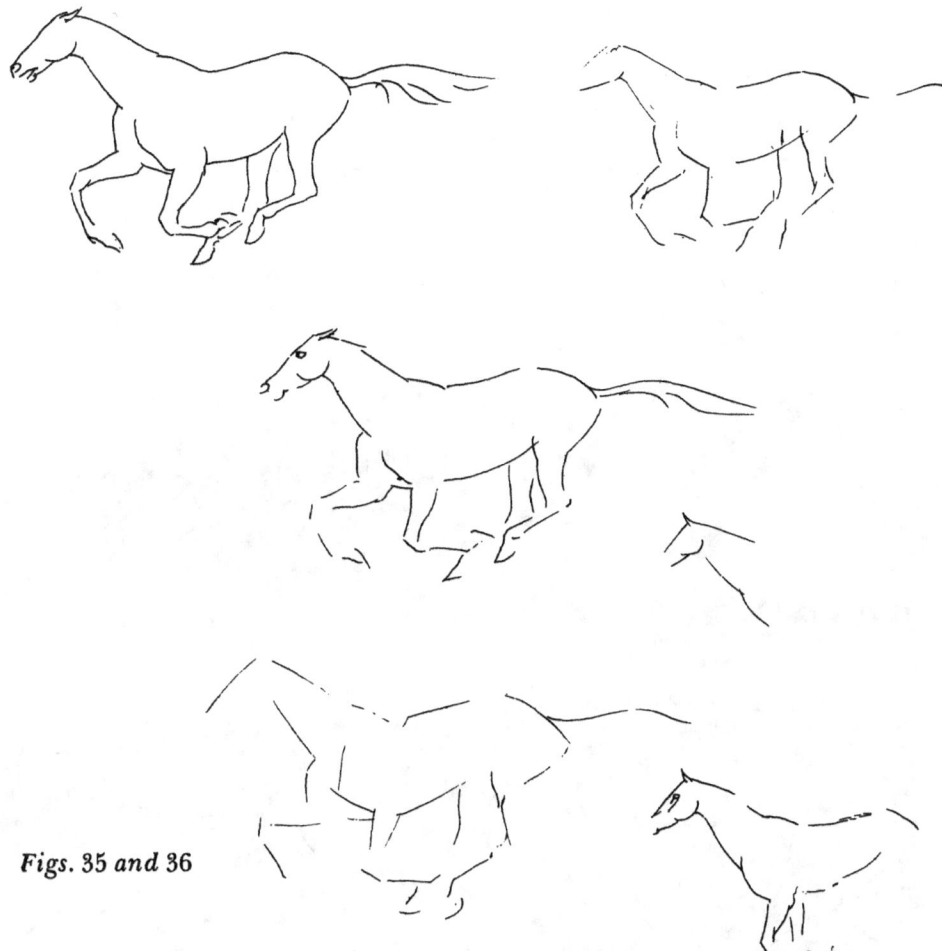

Figs. 35 and 36

QUICK PEN NOTES OF TROTTING
& GALLOPING

47

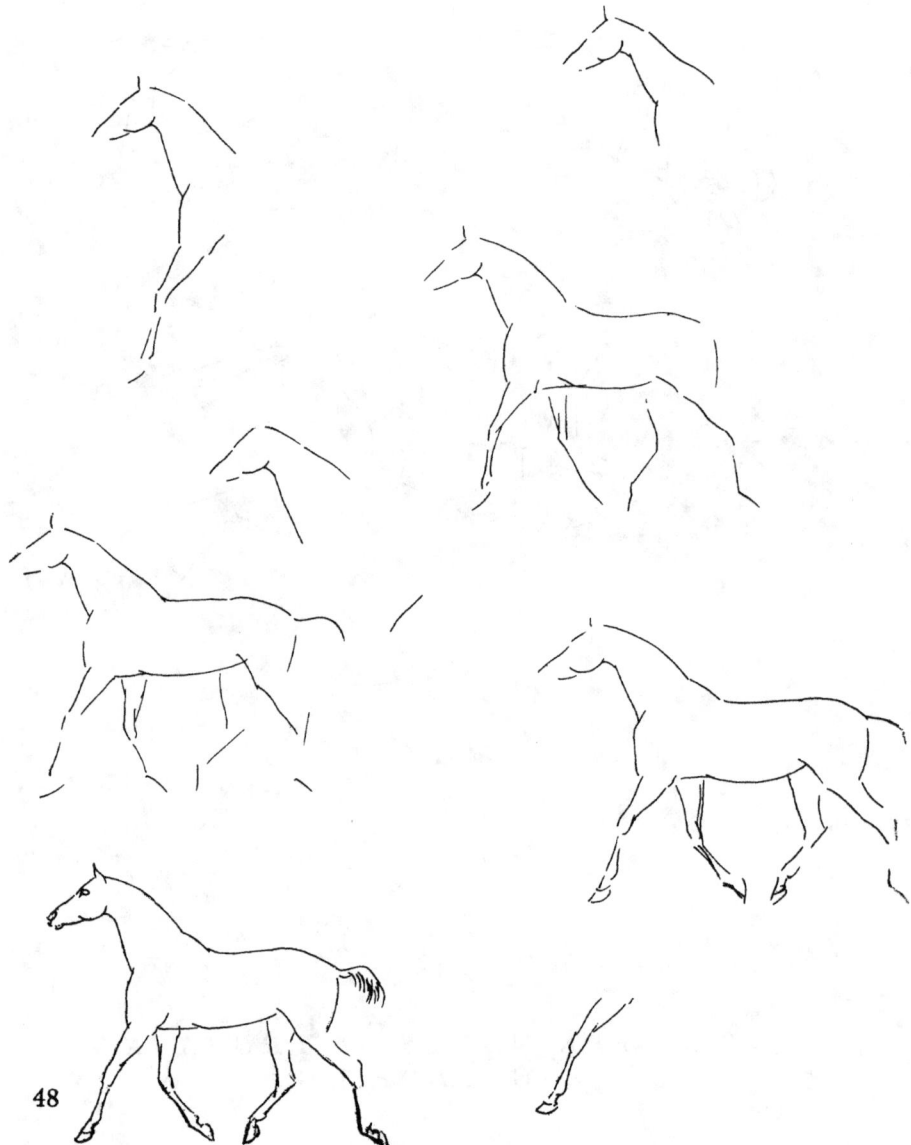

48

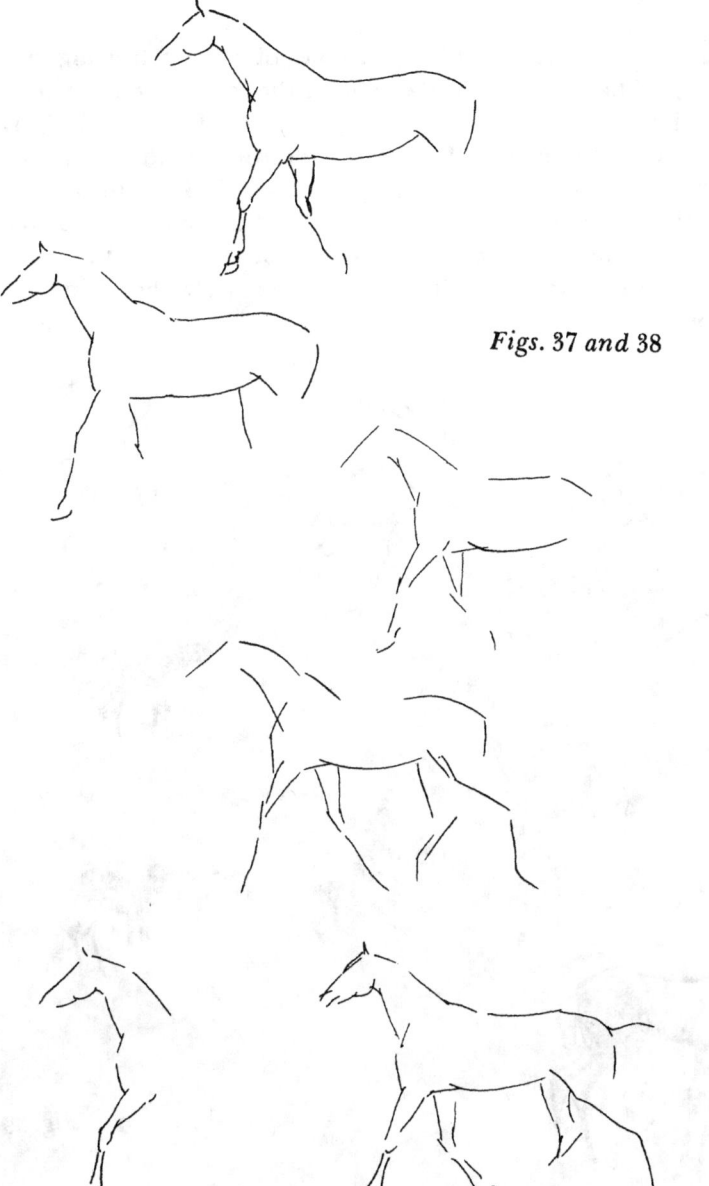

Figs. 37 and 38

49

(Figs. 35-8) These are quick pen notes of a horse trotting and galloping. I have drawn on the edge of the forms here, but they are not intended to be drawings of the horse's form so much as diagrams of his position. The correct position of the body and legs were my only concern. The final drawing, for which these were only mechanical notes, was completed at home. It doesn't matter what sort of drawings you make for studies of this kind as long as they explain quite clearly to yourself the points in question.

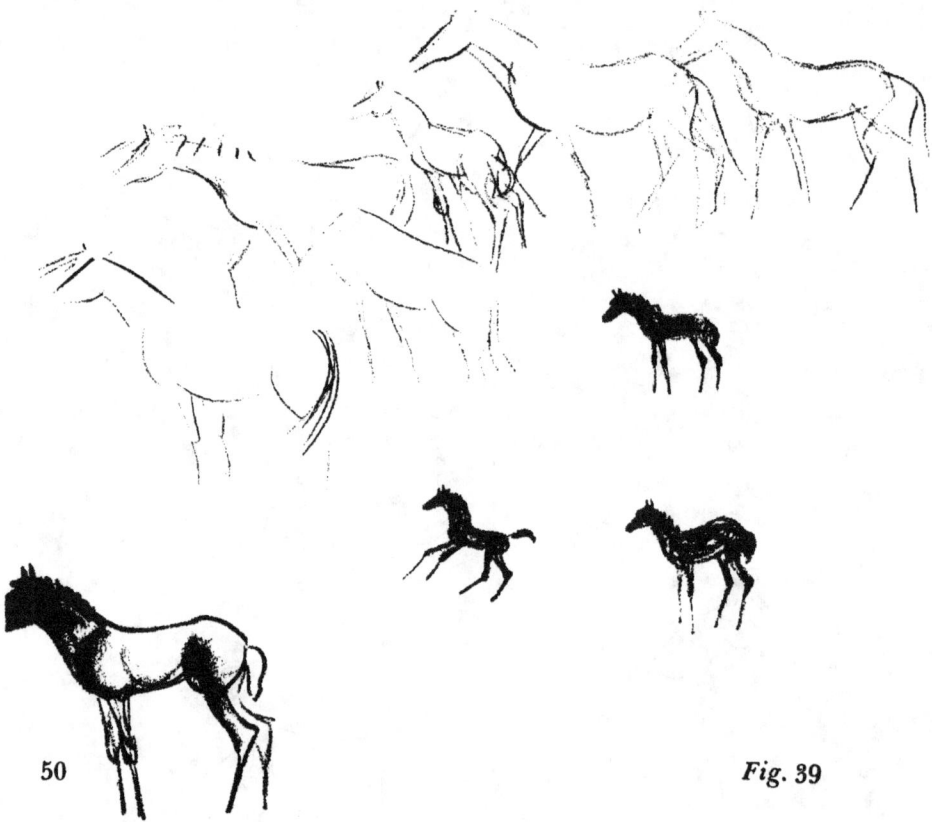

50

Fig. 39

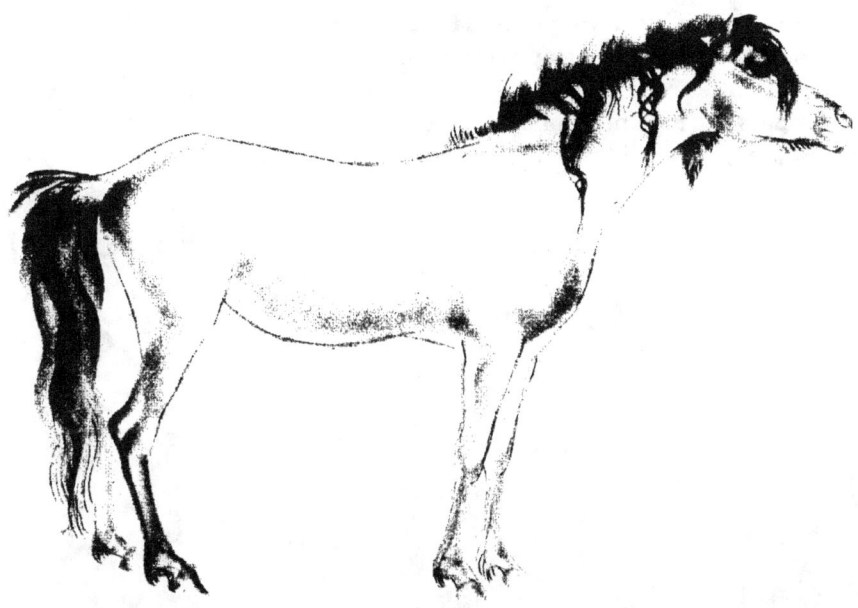

Fig. 40

When the Moorland Ponies have young foals in the herd they are very shy and difficult to approach, and it is impossible to get within two or three hundred yards of them before they move off. This is very annoying because they are lovely subjects for drawing. (Fig. 39) This is a rough note of such a herd. Although the drawing itself is not very good, the fact of making it helped me to memorize some of the important points about these animals. (Fig. 40) When these foals get to be two year olds they lose the charm of the younger animals and are not as good looking as the older ones; most of them are rough and untidy, their manes and tails get matted and full of brambles.

51

(Fig. 41) This is a drawing of a mare and her nine months old foal. The foals sometimes stay around their mothers for two or three years, often one sees a mare with two or three foals of different ages all together; one can then make a comparison of the most important differences between the ages. In all these

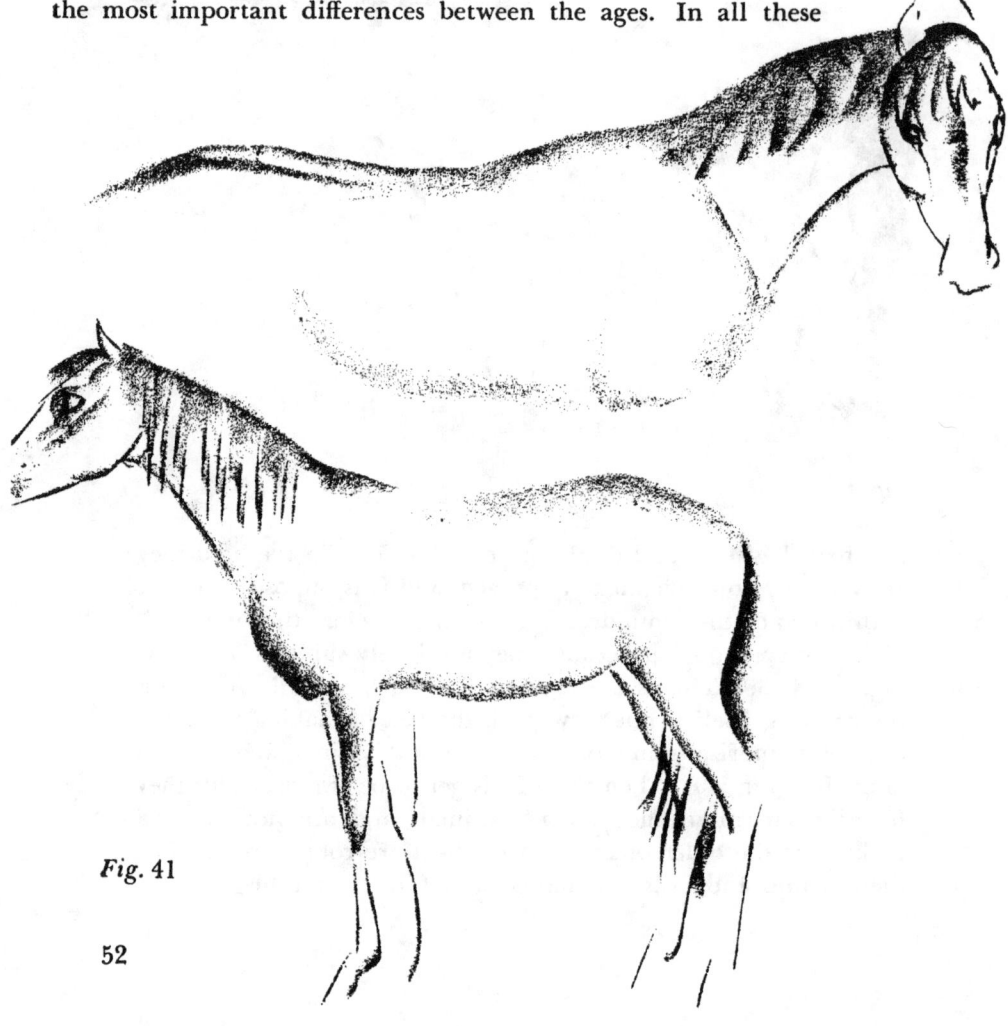

Fig. 41

52

Fig. 42

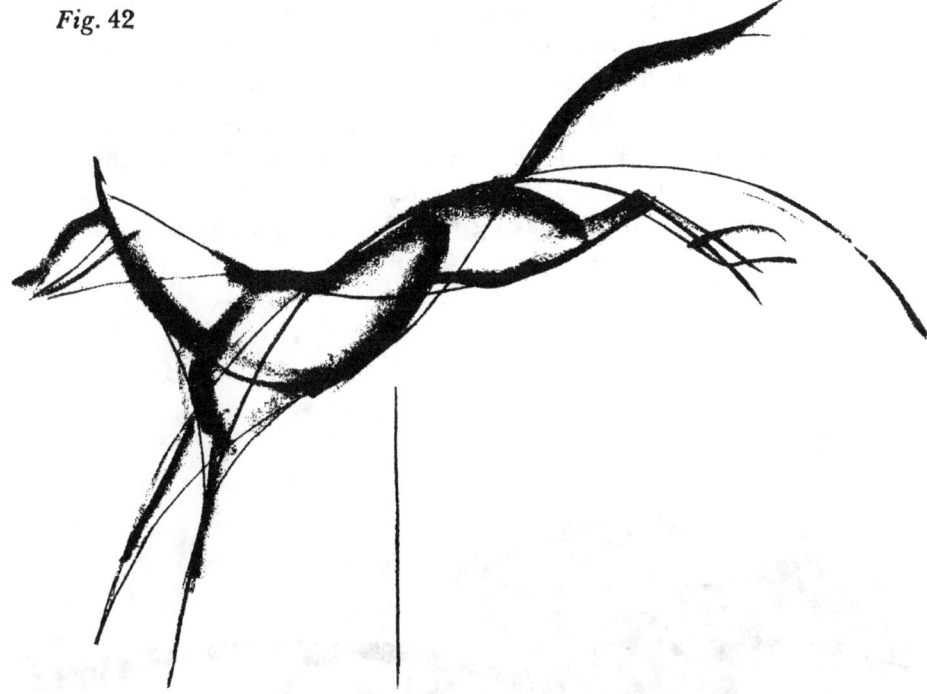

quick sketches I have concentrated on the principal characteristics and movements; that is all one can really do when sketching
out of doors. (Fig. 42) This diagrammatic drawing of a jumping
horse may help you to understand what I mean by movement in
drawing. Arrange the position of your horse so that one form
leads to another in a graceful manner. If you have seen a slow
motion film of horses jumping you will have noticed how the
movements running right from the heads through to the tails
create a beautiful waving effect due to the rhythmic way in
which all the parts are moving together (See also pages 11-18).

(Fig. 43) Get all the vitality possible in your work; it is in this way alone that you will be able to convey your ideas to other people through drawing.

(Fig. 44) Don't confuse what I have described as movement in drawing with the actual position of the animal. I think this drawing has quite a lot of vitality and movement, but the horse is standing still and not making any violent actions at all.

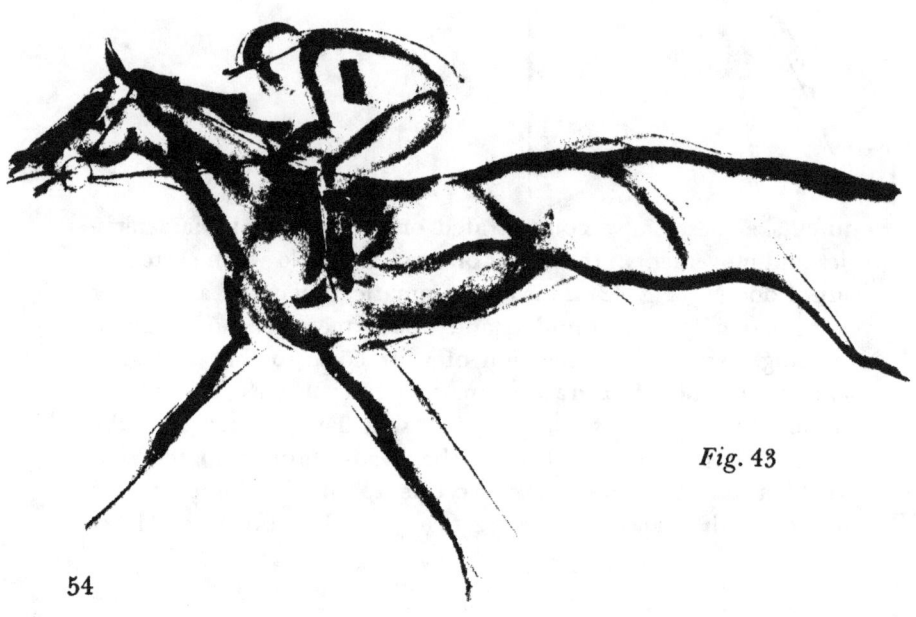

Fig. 43

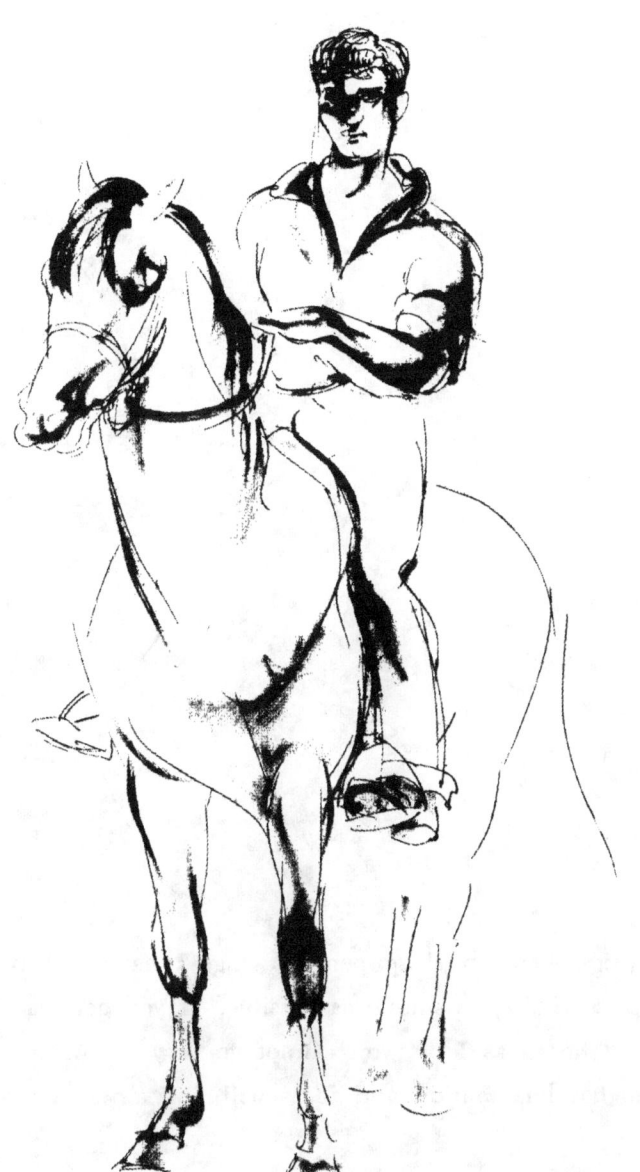

Fig. 44

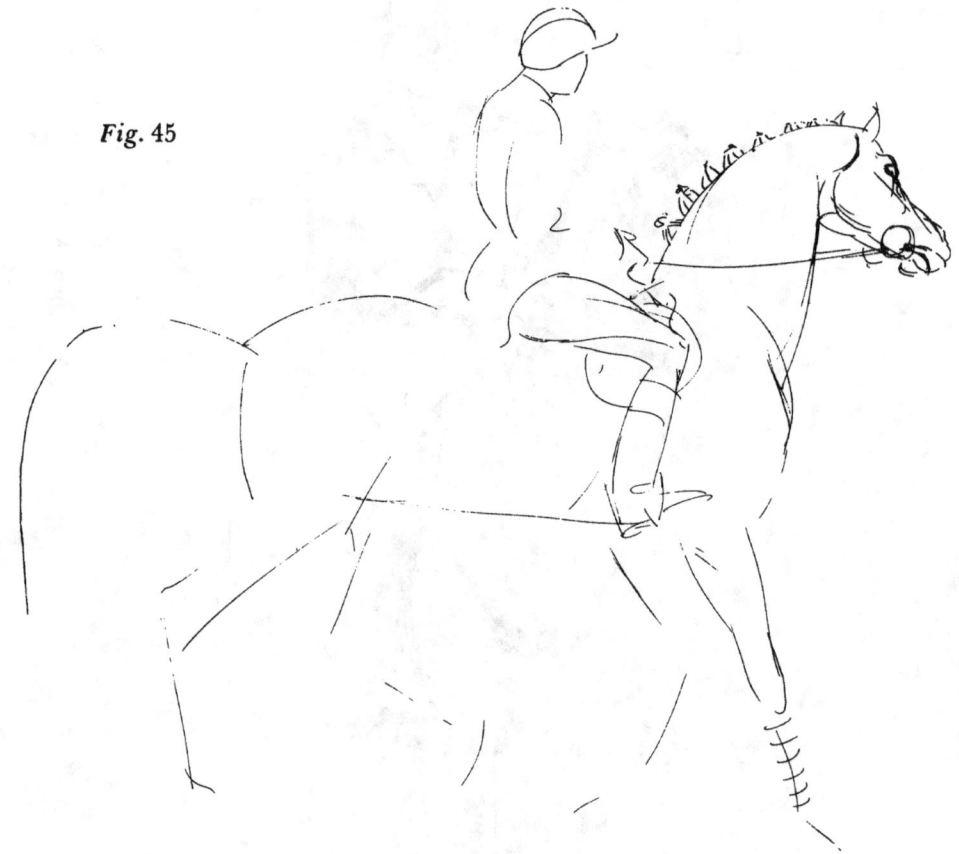

Fig. 45

(Figs. 45-6) In these pen drawings I have endeavoured to express vitality as simple as possible. If you get really excited about horses as I do, you cannot go very far wrong. Anyone who has imagination and ideas will find a way of expressing

56

them. What I have said in this book is naturally limited by the fact that most of the important things about drawing can be expressed in no other way than drawing. After all is said and done, that is why we draw.

Fig. 46

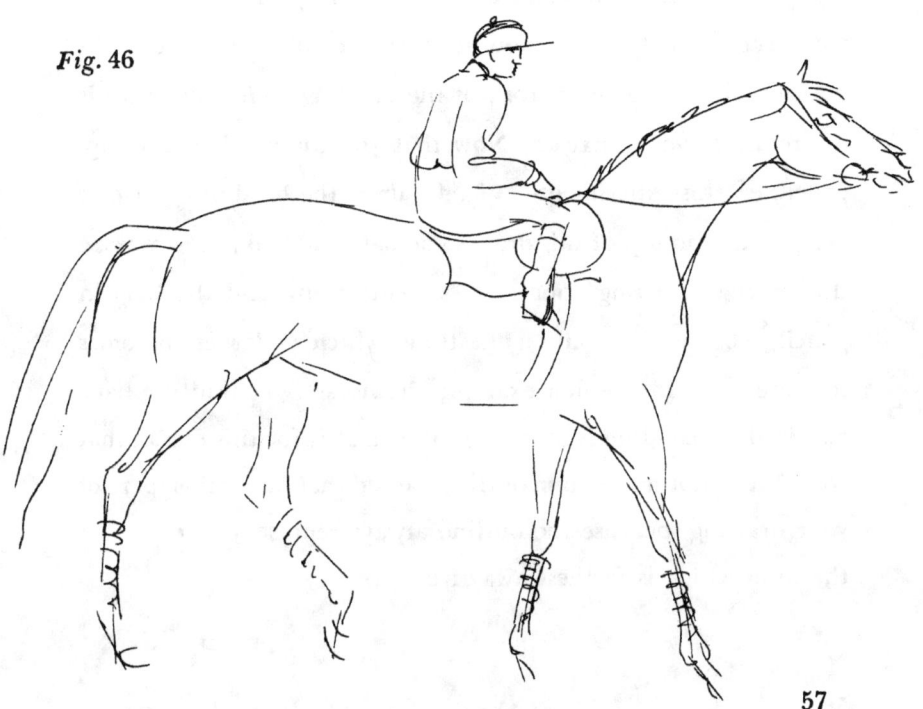

INVENTION AND EXPERIMENT

There is nothing more profitable and enjoyable than experimenting with different materials, and inventing new methods of drawing. Much can be discovered by accident, but if this is to be turned to good account, you must analyse thoroughly each completed drawing, finding the cause of the effects you have obtained. To explain exactly what I mean by analysis:—supposing you have scribbled on a bad drawing, and your scribbled lines are darker than the work you are trying to obliterate, you will notice that they come in front of the drawing. This discovery is the result of your analysis. Now that you know what has happened, try this experiment— (Fig. 47) draw the head of a horse in pencil; and on top of this draw some bars with ink; now reverse this process, drawing your horse's head in ink and the bars in pencil; what is the result? The thing which is darkest becomes the foremost. In the first example the horse is behind the bars, and in the second he is in front of them. It is for this reason that you should not make your outline darker than any other part of your drawing, because the outline always represents the part of the form which is farthest away from you.

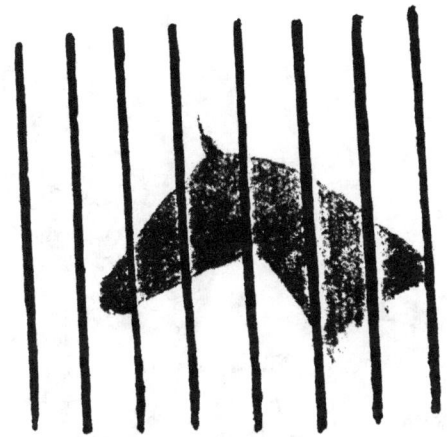

Fig. 47

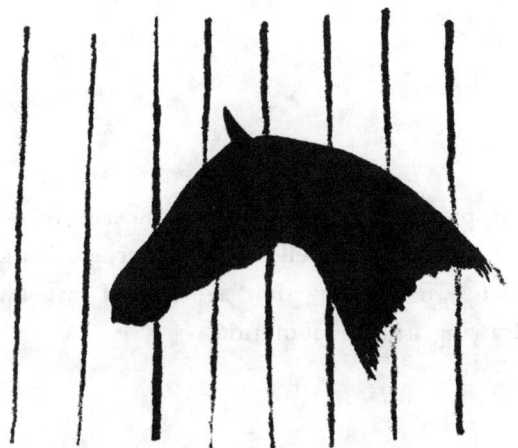

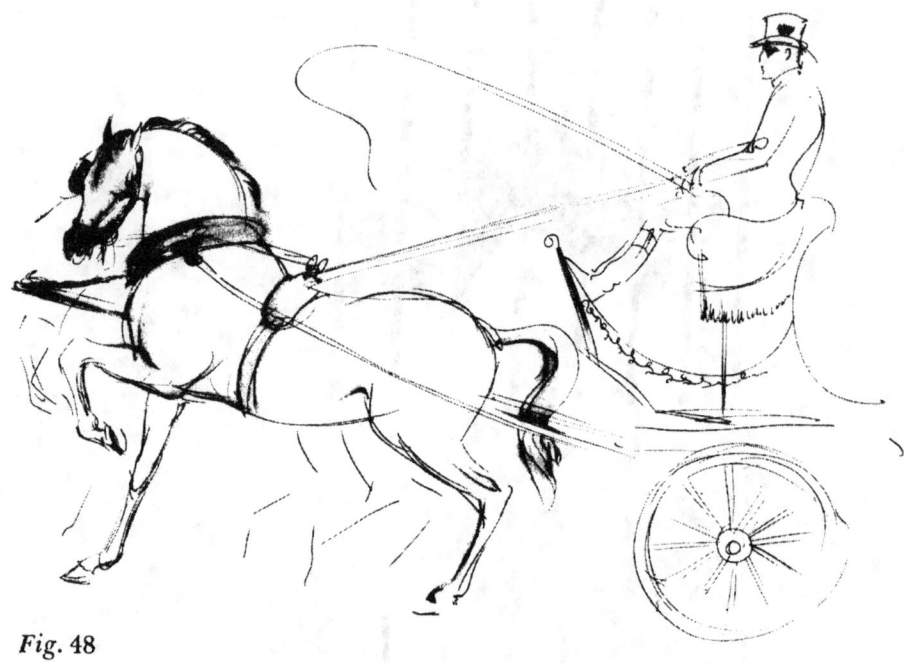

Fig. 48

A carriage and pair can be one of the most lovely sights imaginable, if the horses move well and the carriage is of good design; unfortunately it is a long time ago since I last saw one, so I made this drawing from imagination.

(Fig. 49) As you see these Circus Horses are drawn with a pen and ink, but in the next drawing I applied the ink mostly with

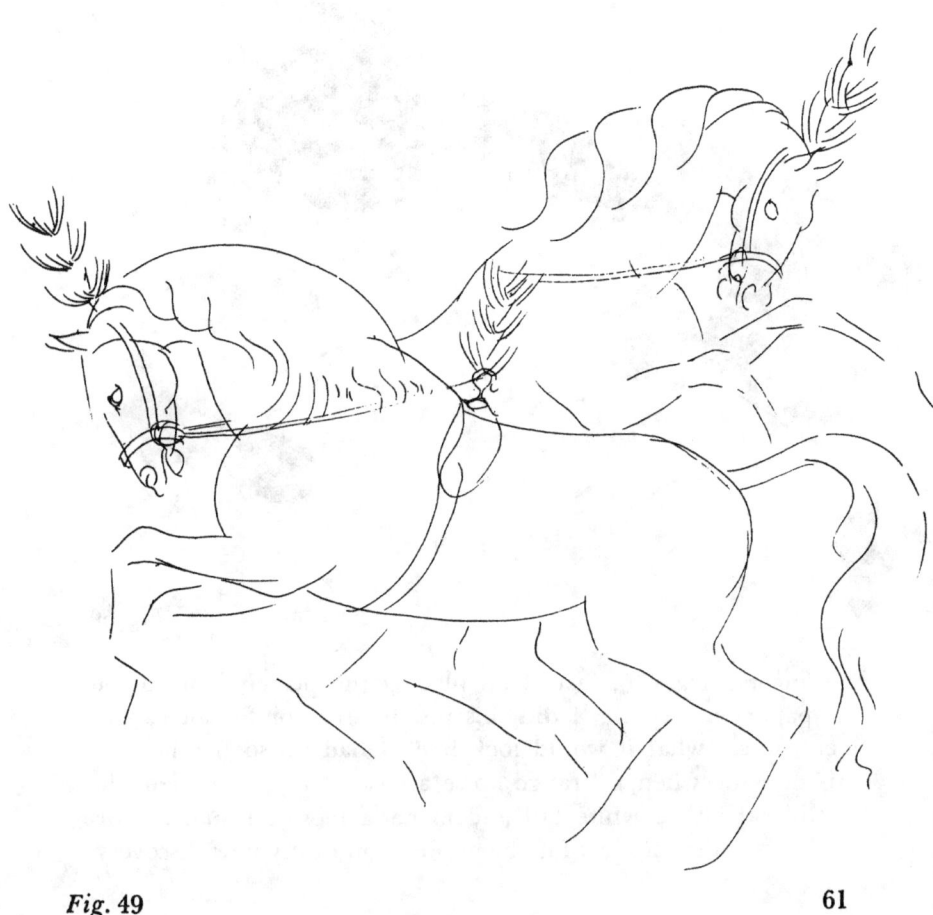

Fig. 49

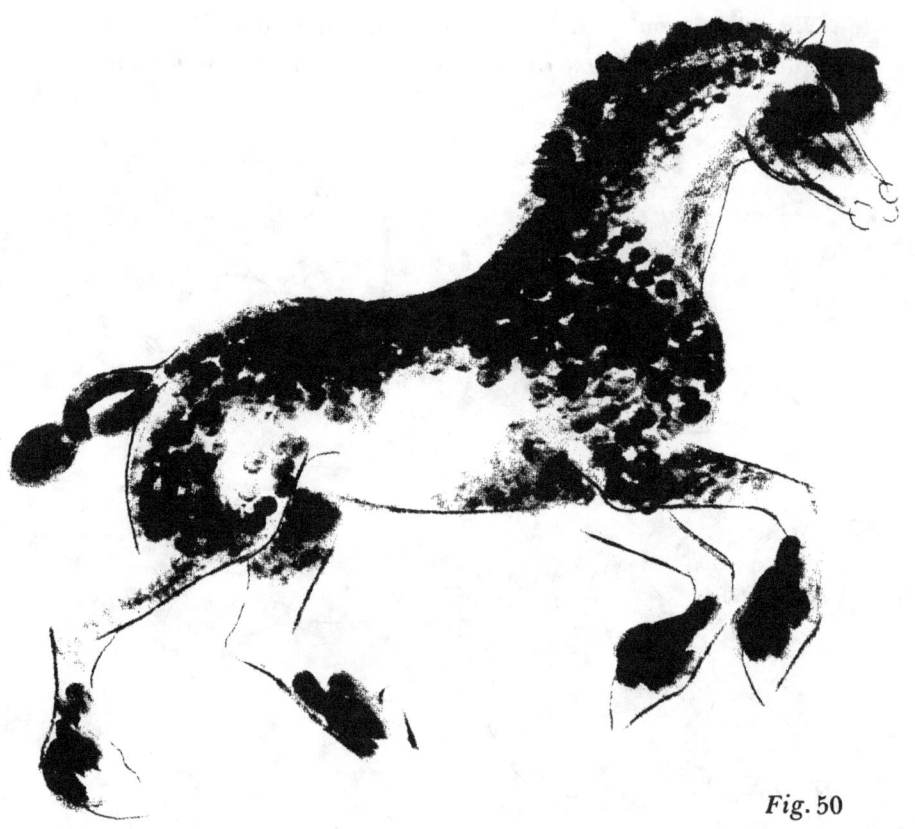

Fig. 50

my fingers (Fig. 50), first of all placing the principal forms on the paper with chalk. I did this just for fun, or for an experiment, to see what it would look like. I had no sooner finished this drawing when a strange horse appeared in the garden; he was black with a white tail and mane, a most unusual colouring but an ideal subject for the application of my new discovery.

62

(Fig. 51) I made this drawing of him almost entirely with my fingers, and I think you will agree with me that the results of this experiment were satisfactory, and proved beyond doubt that drawing for fun is the surest way of obtaining successful results.

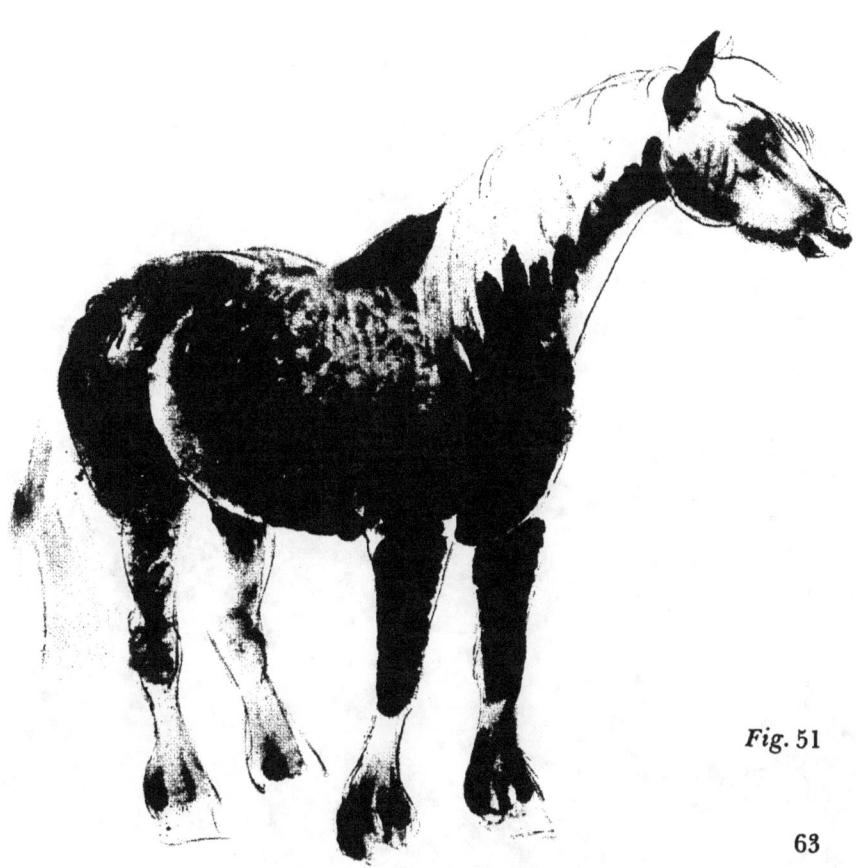

Fig. 51

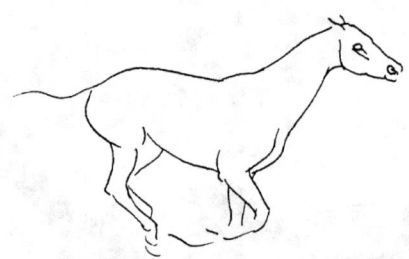

COACHWHIP PUBLICATIONS

COACHWHIPBOOKS.COM

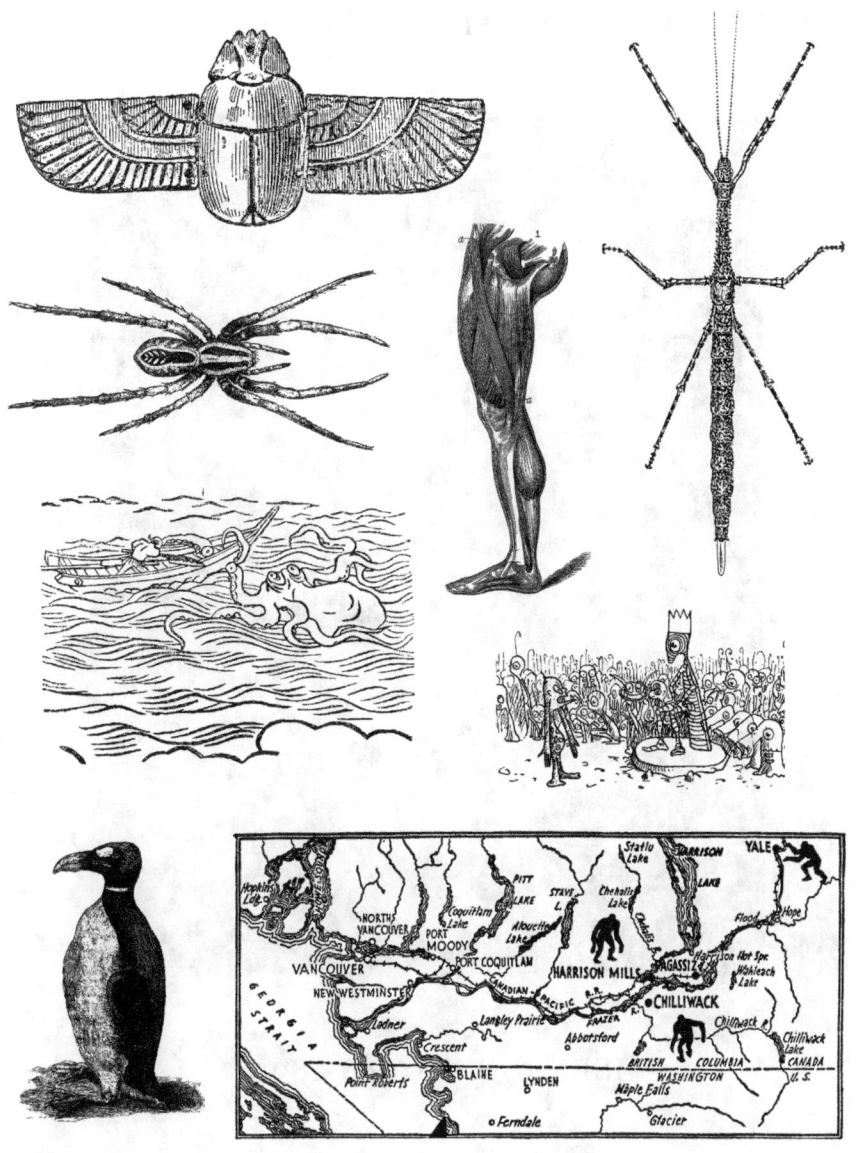

COACHWHIP PUBLICATIONS

COACHWHIPBOOKS.COM

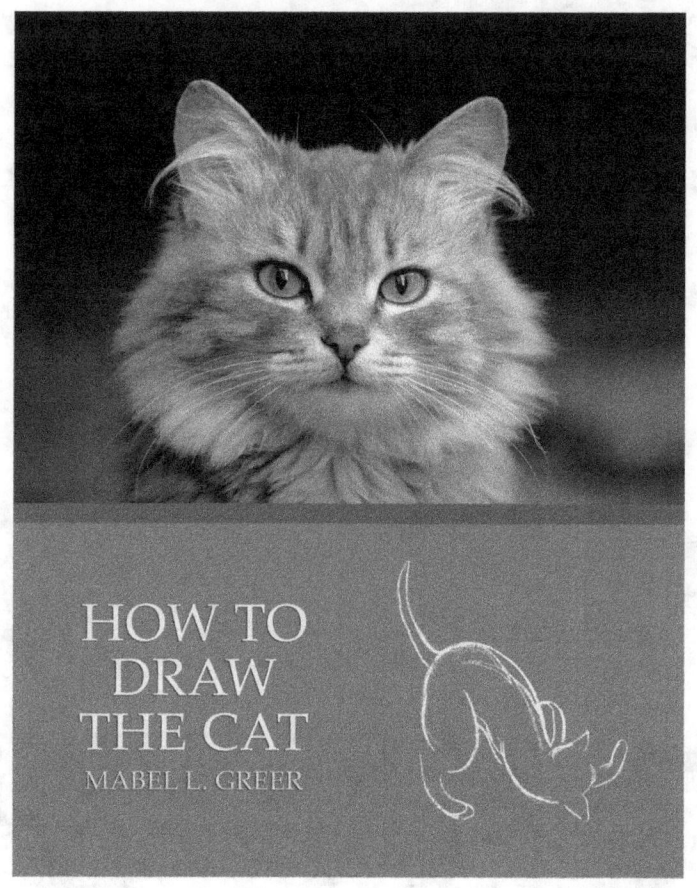

HOW TO
DRAW
THE CAT
MABEL L. GREER

ISBN 978-1-61646-189-8

COACHWHIP PUBLICATIONS

COACHWHIPBOOKS.COM

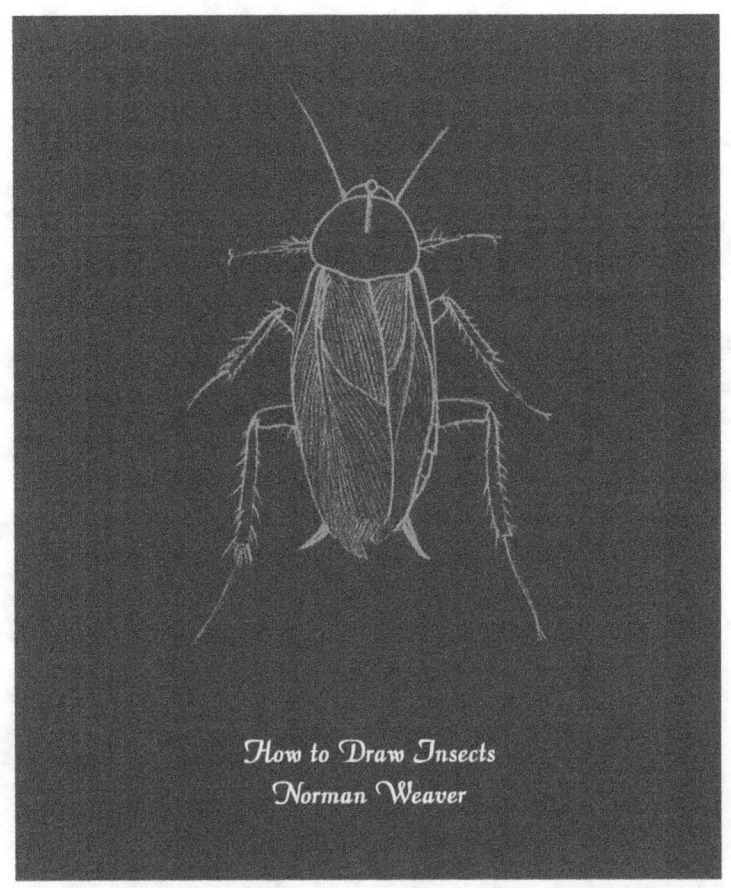

How to Draw Insects
Norman Weaver

ISBN 978-1-61646-191-1

www.ingramcontent.com/pod-product-compliance
Lightning Source LLC
Chambersburg PA
CBHW081304170526
45165CB00011B/3401